DEVELOPING
A
SERVANT'S
HEART

CHARLES
STANLEY

OLIVER
NELSON

THOMAS NELSON PUBLISHERS
Nashville

Published in Nashville, Tennessee, by Thomas Nelson, Inc., Publishers, and distributed in Canada by Word Communications, Ltd., Richmond, British Columbia

The Bible version used in this publication is THE NEW KING JAMES VERSION. Copyright © 1979, 1980, 1982, Thomas Nelson, Inc., Publishers.

ISBN 0-7852-7279-8

Printed in the United States of America

CONTENTS

THE REASON FOR YOUR SALVATION

How would you complete the following three statements?

1. God saved me because ___He loves me___.

2. God's purpose for saving me was ___Reflect His Glory___

3. I am most like Jesus when I ___HAVE A SERVANT'S HEART___

The purpose for my opening this Bible study with a little quiz is not to put you on the spot, but rather to set the proper framework for our discussion of servanthood. The answers that I am seeking to these statements are these:

God Saved Me Because *He Loves Me*

The sole reason that God sent His Son, Jesus, to this world to die for your sins and mine was because He loved us. God forgives us, grants us eternal life, and gives us the gift of His Holy Spirit out of His immeasurable love and grace. There is no other reason.

Many people seem to believe that God saves a man or woman because of the person's good works or service. Nothing could be farther from the truth. There isn't any amount or any type of service that can earn salvation. The apostle Paul made this very clear when he wrote to the Ephesians: "For by grace you have been saved through faith, and that not of yourselves; it is the gift of God, not of works, lest anyone should boast" (Eph. 2:8–9). Even the faith by which we believe God forgives us and saves us is a gift of God that flows from His love!

If God saved a person on the basis of works, we each would have to ask ourselves, "How much good service is enough?" Such a question cannot be answered. There is no amount of good service that can equal the shed blood of Jesus Christ. There is no way to quantify how much service is necessary for salvation or to qualify which types of service lead to salvation. The gospel is: Jesus Christ shed His blood on the cross of Calvary to purchase salvation for you and for me. He did so voluntarily and willingly in obedience to His heavenly Father, who was completely and totally motivated by love when He sought your redemption and mine. John 3:16 tells us, "For God so *loved* the world that He gave His only begotten Son, that whoever believes in Him should not perish but have everlasting life."

Just as a person is not saved because of his past good works, neither is a person saved because he has potential for future good works. God does not look at one person and say, "You have the potential to be a preacher, so I am going to save you" and then look at another and say, "You aren't worth much, so I won't save you." God's gift of salvation is offered freely to all who will receive it. God created each one of us with a unique set of talents and traits that can be employed for His service as He wills. No person is without merit in His eyes; all are worthy of salvation.

Equally so, there is no inherent "goodness" in any person that warrants his or her salvation. No person has the prerogative to stand before God Almighty and say, "I deserve to be saved." Rather, we each must confess, "I *need* to be saved." Romans 3:23 says, "For all have sinned and fall short of the glory of God." All means *all*.

This point is critical for you to understand at the outset of this study on service: Developing a servant's heart is something that we do in *response* to God's gracious gifts of salvation, eternal life, and the Holy Spirit. It is never something that we do in order to *earn*—win, warrant, or put ourselves into a position to deserve—salvation.

Reflect His Glory

God's Purpose for Saving Me Was *to Bring Him Glory*

God saved you and He saved me so that we might be His "trophies"—we might be examples to others of God's love and mercy at work in and through a human life.

Many people seem to think that the only reason for salvation is so that a person might go to heaven when he dies. Eternal life is part of God's forgiveness plan for us, but that is not the sole reason for our salvation. We are saved so that we might be "redeemed"—a word that implies that we once were in bondage or slavery to something that was evil, but we have been rescued and set free from sin so that we might live a life of righteousness before God. If God's only purpose for our salvation was so that we might go to heaven, He would be doing each of us a great favor by saving us and then immediately slaying us.

God's purpose for saving us is so that we each might reflect His nature—we might be His people on this earth, doing the kinds of works that Jesus Himself would do if He were walking in our shoes, through our world, during our lifetime. God desires to manifest His character through our personalities and giftedness. When we allow His Holy Spirit to work in us and through us to others, we become vessels of His love in action. We reflect His compassion, love, and mercy to others. And in so doing, we are His witnesses. We bring credit, honor, and glory to *Him*.

God does not save us in order that we might be part of an elite group of "good people." He saves us in order that we might reach out to all people with God's goodness. He does not put us in the church so that we might soak up several decades of good sermons, Bible conferences, prayer meetings, and seminars. He puts us in the church so that we might be of good use to those who are in need—so that we might function as His body, each of us using our gifts, talents, and skills as the Holy Spirit directs to help one another, and in the process, experience a refinement of our own spirits, souls, and minds.

This is an important point for you to consider as we begin this Bible study. God did not save you simply so that you can say to others, "I'm saved," that you might fill out a church membership card, or that you might have the assurance that you are going to heaven one day. He saved you in order that you might live every hour of every day of the remainder of your life in faithful service and obedience to Jesus Christ—going wherever He leads, saying and doing whatever He prompts you to say and do by His Holy Spirit, and engaging in whatever forms of ministry and service that He calls you to pursue.

I Am Most Like Jesus When I *Serve Others*

The foremost characteristic of the life of Jesus Christ was and is *service.* We are most like Him when we serve as He served.

Many seem to think that a person is most like Jesus when he preaches as Jesus preached, teaches as Jesus taught, heals as Jesus healed, or performs miracles as Jesus performed miracles. They look only at the outward manifestation of a person's witness and ministry.

They need to look beyond the outer manifestation to the *motivation* for Jesus' life. That motivation was always *service.* Jesus preached, taught, healed, and performed miracles in order to help others, never to call attention to Himself. He poured out His very life so that others might be saved, never thinking for a moment to save Himself. Time and again, Jesus said to those He had healed or helped, "Don't tell anyone what has happened." The reason for this was that Jesus didn't want others to respond to Him as an earthly political savior. He didn't want them to focus on His potential to rule over them, but, rather, to focus on our loving heavenly Father and on Jesus' role to serve humanity as Savior, Deliverer, and Redeemer.

The critical point for us to recognize at the outset of this study is this: God has called you to serve others just as Jesus served others. He didn't save you or call you to service so that you might be exalted, praised, glorified, or put on a pedestal. He saved you so that you might serve others and in so doing, bring praise and honor to God's holy name.

The good news is that any person who is saved *can* serve God and bring glory to Him. The nature of the ministry task or calling is not what is important; what *is* important is the motivation behind our service. God loved us so that we might love others. That's what the Christian life is all about.

Having a clear understanding about why God saved you and what He expects of you may very well be the most important aspect of this entire study. As you prepare to engage in this Bible study, ask yourself these important questions:

•*What do I expect from God now that I'm saved?*

Security in Him - Power with Him (to overcome sin) - A ministry like His (touching others)

• *On what grounds do I base that expectation?*

Scriptures - I know the future I have for you Greater is He in you - Go ye into all the world

•*What do I expect from myself as a Christian?*

To have discernment - wisdom - love - and effectiveness

•*What does God expect from me as His faithful and obedient child?*

Surrender obedience to seek to know Him.

LESSON 1

A FRESH PERSPECTIVE ON SERVANTHOOD

The Bible is far more than a great piece of literature or a book of inspirational and spiritual truths. It is a very practical manual for daily living. In many ways, it is God's "Service Manual" for life. It tells us how to live a godly life, how to maintain loving relationships, and how to fulfill our reason for being on this earth. The Bible relates to every area of our lives. It clearly tells us how to use all of our resources—our gifts, time, talents, money, possessions, and skills—for God's glory and His purposes, which are the foundation and motivation for all forms of ministry and servanthood.

From cover to cover, the Bible is filled with examples of men and women who had a servant's heart and who demonstrated loving service to others. So often, however, we tend to focus on what these people *did*—and especially the miracles of God that may have accompanied their deeds—rather than on the fact that virtually all of the great stories in the Bible are examples that fall into one of three categories:

1. God's service to mankind
2. Mankind's service to God

3. The service of men and women to other men and women

Service is *giving*. And giving is the very essence of the gospel. God *gave* His only begotten Son. Jesus *gave* His life on the cross. We *give* our hearts to God. We, in turn, are called to *give* of ourselves to others.

It is easy to read the Bible and think, *Isn't it wonderful what that great Bible hero or heroine did or experienced?* In so doing, we rarely think that the Bible story or example has anything to do with us personally. The better question to ask is this: "What is it that God desires for me to do or experience?" The fact is, God intends for each of us to

- be the recipient of His ongoing giving to us,
- be the giver of ongoing praise and worship to God, and
- be the giver of good gifts of all types to those with whom we have daily contact or are called to serve.

The Bible tells us not only what to expect when we serve others, but how to serve others. And beyond that, it challenges us to serve with great generosity and unconditional love.

As you study God's principles for servanthood and ways in which you might better develop a genuine servant's heart, I encourage you to go again and again to your Bible for inspiration as well as guidance. Underline phrases. Highlight words or verses. Make notes in the margins of your Bible to record the specific ways God speaks to you.

God's truth is for all people at all times, but the application of that truth to your life is always very personal and direct. Be open to the specific ways in which God admonishes, encourages, or directs *you* to serve Him and to serve others.

For Group or Personal Study

This book can be used by you alone or by several people in a small-group or Sunday-school-class study. If you are using this book for personal study, you will find places from time to time where you will be asked to record your insights or respond to questions. If you are using the book for a small-group study, you may also use these questions and insight portions to prompt group discussion.

At various times, you will be asked to relate to the material in one of these four ways:

1. What new insights have you gained?
2. Have you ever had a similar experience?
3. How do you feel about the material presented?
4. In what way do you feel challenged to respond or to act?

Insights

An insight occurs when you see something that you haven't seen before or you have a new understanding about something. Insights relate to *meaning*. You have a new spiritual insight when you gain a deeper meaning for what God's Word is saying to you.

Many of us have had the experience of reading a passage of the Bible and saying, "I never saw that before. I never noticed that particular word or phrase in the way I have just noticed it. I have a new understanding of that story or teaching." You may have studied or meditated on the passage in the past, but suddenly, God moves you to a deeper level of understanding. That is a spiritual insight.

Insights tend to be highly personal. We see the truths of the Bible in the light of our personal experiences, past and present. At times, insights help us as we reflect upon a relationship or incident that we are facing presently or will be facing in the immediate future. At other times, an insight helps answer a question, confirm a belief, or provide a sudden knowing about what we must do.

Ask the Lord to speak to you personally every time you study your Bible. I believe He will answer your prayer. I also believe the insights He gives you will cause you to have a growing enthusiasm for studying His Word.

Make notes about the insights you have. You may want to record them in your Bible or in a separate journal. As you reflect back over your insights, you are likely to see, over time, how God has moved in your life and how He is causing you to grow spiritually. In my experience, I have found that the more I record insights, the more insights I have.

From time to time in this book, you will be asked to reflect upon what a particular passage of Scripture says to you. These are times for recording your personal insights, not for summarizing a group response or for writing down what someone else in your Bible-study group may say. Make sure the insights or responses you record flow from your own heart and experience.

Experience

Each of us approaches the Bible from a unique background—our own particular set of relationships and experiences. We each have our own set of ideas, opinions, and emotions. Therefore, we each have a unique perspective on what we read in God's Word.

Different levels of experience may create problems in a group Bible study, although this is not necessarily the case. People who have gone to church all their lives and have heard Bible stories and good preaching since their childhood may have a different depth of understanding of the Bible from those who are new Christians or who have never read God's Word. Be sensitive to the differences that may exist in your group. Don't let a beginner feel lost or unimportant. If you are an "old-timer," don't become impatient.

What we each have in common are life experiences. Each of us can point to times in which we have found the Bible to be directly applicable to us—perhaps to convict us or challenge us, or to comfort and encourage us in times of trouble. We have had experiences about which we can say, "I know God was really speaking to *me* from His Word because that passage of Scripture is *exactly* what I needed or was about what I once experienced."

Our experiences do not make the Bible true. The Word of God is truth regardless of our opinion about it or our experiences with it. It is important, however, to note and share our experiences for this reason: We begin to see how God's truth can be applied to human lives and circumstances, and in the process, our faith grows. We gain a new awareness of how personally and directly God speaks to each person through the Bible. The Word of God comes alive to us as we see it meeting practical needs, answering questions, and addressing specific situations. We discover that God's Word is not only universal—for every person in every generation and every culture—but also very specific to individuals, times, and places. A person who has a broad experience of sharing Bible-related experiences with other Christians nearly always comes to the conclusion that our greatest potential for harmony and unity in the church lies in each person's having a relationship with Christ Jesus and then living a life based upon agreement with God's Word. The Lord and His Word bind us together with bonds that cannot be broken.

If you are doing this study on your own, find someone with whom you can share your faith experiences. Be open to hearing about that person's faith experiences in return.

Emotional Response

Just as each of us has a personal inventory of life experiences, so each of us has a range of emotional responses. Allow others in your Bible-study group to share their emotional responses to God's Word without comment or judgment. You may feel overjoyed or encouraged after reading a passage of Scripture. Another person may respond to that same passage with conviction, questions, or fear. No one emotion is the "right" emotion to feel.

Face your emotions honestly. Learn to share your emotional responses with others as candidly and as thoroughly as you can. You will learn more about yourself, and also more about the way God intends for emotions to operate for our benefit.

Service to others can be a very emotion-laden topic. There are those who feel great compassion for others and can hardly keep from crying when they hear about needs, or from moving to respond to them. There are others who are much more stoic and objective. They see a need, they address it, they do their utmost to resolve it solely because they know it is the right thing to do. In both cases, people are serving God in their service to others! Successful service is not limited to highly emotional people or to those who can show great empathy. Feeling empathy and displaying emotion are often two different things.

Emotional responses do not give validity to the Scriptures, nor should we trust our emotions as a gauge for our faith. Faith is to be based on what God says, not on how we feel. We must remain balanced in our understanding of emotions: On the one hand, we each have an emotional response to God's Word and to our having a relationship with God and others; on the other, we must not let our emotions rule our interpretation of God's Word or limit us to reading only those passages that make us feel happy and hopeful.

I strongly believe that in small-group Bible study it is more beneficial for participants to express their emotions than to give their opinions. Some of the ways in which God speaks to us through His Word are nonverbal. The Holy Spirit often communicates with us through the unspoken language of intuition, emotions, desires, and longings. When we share feelings with one another, we not only open ourselves to insights into God's Word, but we also grow closer to other members of the body of Christ. A sense of community develops, and we gain a deeper understanding of what it means to be "one in the Spirit." It is through the sharing of joys and sorrows, assurances and doubts, hopes and fears, that we mature as individuals and as churches.

The sharing of opinions often divides people. Opinions tend to polarize and categorize. The sharing of emotional responses does just the opposite. Be very sensitive to what happens when a person says, "I think thus and so about this verse." There is a much greater reception to a person and to the moving of God's Spirit if a person will say, "This verse causes me to feel this way."

Scholarly commentaries and factual information have their place in Bible study, but the more beneficial contribution to the group process is still likely to be the sharing of emotional responses. A small-group Bible study is not a forum for exchanging information; it is an opportunity to build faith within a community of believers.

Challenges

As we read God's Word, we nearly always come to a point of conviction when we feel certain that God is speaking directly to us. I once heard this described by one person as an "oh me, oh my" experience. Another person once said, "God has my name on that verse." Those are just two ways that a challenge or conviction may strike you.

God's Word may cause you to feel inspired or challenged to change something in your life, to make a fresh start, or to take a new step. At other times, you may feel challenged to stand firm in your resolve or to continue steadfastly in the direction you are going. These challenges may be very strong. They may occur once or repeatedly, but they are virtually impossible to ignore or escape. The more practical the subject matter, the stronger the convictions seem to be. That may be because God's message and meaning are so clear that there is little room to explain away, justify, or misinterpret what God is saying to you.

Don't dismiss or downgrade the challenges you feel. Take them seriously and find ways of acting upon them.

This is especially important in your development of a servant's heart. If God reveals to you a particular need that He desires for *you* to address, calls you to a particular avenue of ministry, or brings to your mind a specific need or situation, take that as "marching orders" from God. Don't simply close your Bible, close this study book, and walk away feeling either elated or deflated. God is expecting you to *do* something with the challenge He has just given you. Make certain, of course, that your final action plan is based on a complete understanding of God's principles and plan. You may need to engage in one or more interim steps as you seek to fulfill God's call to service in your life. Nevertheless, start on those steps. Don't procrastinate or second-guess God's challenge to you.

Again, I encourage you to write down the ways in which you believe God is stretching, molding, calling, or guiding you. It is when we clearly identify and succinctly state what we believe God wants us to do that we nearly always can identify the next step that is required of us. Our response to God's challenge will become more responsible, measured, and deliberate. We are to *respond* to God's Word, not merely react to it.

God's ultimate plan is to get His Word into us and us into His Word so we can take His Word into the world, live it out, and be witnesses of His Word in all we say and do. Our purpose is not to absorb sermons, but to become "living sermons" of God's truth to all who touch our lives. It is not enough to note insights, recall past experiences, share emotions, or write down the ways in which we feel challenged. We must obey God's Word and be doers of it (James 1:22).

Very specifically, it isn't enough for you to recognize that God is calling you to develop a servant's heart, or even for you to develop a heart for others. You are called by God to engage in active service to others. Do what it is that God is calling *you* to do as His servant in your particular church, community, or sphere of influence.

Keep the Bible Central

Again, I caution you to keep the Bible at the center of your study. Perhaps because they are spiritual in nature, Bible-study groups sometimes become therapy or support groups. While there is great value to those types of groups, that is *not* what a true Bible study accomplishes. A genuine Bible study stays focused on God's Word and promotes a growing faith and a closer walk with the Holy Spirit in *each* person who participates.

Also guard against a tendency to use a group for a soapbox to tell about your own pet concerns, projects, or groups. The Bible-study group is not a place to recruit others to your cause, committee, or organization.

Think of the Bible as your banquet table. Keep it as your focal point for spiritual nourishment and your place for spiritual fellowship. You can best "serve" the other members of your Bible-study group by keeping the Bible and the love of Christ Jesus your primary concerns.

Begin and End in Prayer

I encourage you to start and conclude your Bible study sessions in prayer. Ask God to give you spiritual eyes to see what He wants you to see and spiritual ears to hear what He wants you to hear. Ask Him to give you new insights, to recall to your memory the experiences that are helpful to your growth, and to help you clarify and share your emotions. Be bold in asking God to reveal to you in His Word what He desires for you to take as the next step in your development of a servant's heart.

As you conclude your study, ask the Lord to seal to your mind and heart what you have learned so that you will never forget it and be quick to apply it. Ask Him to help you grow into the fullness of the stature of Christ Jesus—the supreme Servant!

The Depth of God's Word

Avoid the temptation at the conclusion of your ten-lesson study to think that you have all the information necessary to be a successful servant of the Lord Jesus Christ. We each grow in our ability to serve until the day we die. We are called to continue to explore ways in which we might be more and more effective in the way we minister to the needs of others. Our ability to serve is directly related to our spiritual maturity. Be open to ways in which God desires to use you that are *beyond* anything you have done in the past, and very likely beyond anything that you thought He might ever call you to do.

Never stop exploring the riches of God's Word on any topic. I can guarantee you without any hesitation that as you remain faithful in reading God's Word on a daily basis and in obeying what it is that God challenges you to do, you will have a much greater understanding a year from now about what it means to be a servant of Christ Jesus.

• *What new insights about servanthood do you anticipate God may have for you personally and individually? Is there something specific that you hope to gain from this study?*

Humility practical applications
Forgiveness of others As I see my short-
comings

• *In what areas have you struggled with the concept of service, ministry, or God's calling in the past?*

Acting on a service Opening my
home (laziness / pride)

- *How do you feel about service or ministry to others? Is the concept of servanthood frightening to you? How do you feel about engaging in a ministry outreach to others in need?*

I WANT TO BE DISCIPLINED I WANT TO BE FAITHFUL AND NOT GROW WEARY

- *In what ways do you feel challenged by the idea of servanthood or ministry?*

TIME Restrictions IMPATIENCE

LESSON 2

CALLED TO BE A SERVANT

Jesus came as a servant, not as a superstar. His three-year ministry was a powerful example of servanthood—from His first miracle of changing water to wine at a wedding feast to His sacrificial death on the cross in which His own blood flowed freely for the salvation of all who would believe in Him and receive God's offer of forgiveness from sins.

Jesus made two great statements about servanthood that were not only references to His own life and sacrificial death, but words that are related to our role as servants today.

Planted Like Wheat

In the days immediately preceding His crucifixion, Jesus spoke candidly with His disciples about His impending death and resurrection. Much of what He said they didn't understand fully at the time He spoke to them; looking back, however, they understood very clearly the meaning of His words.

John tells in his Gospel about an incident that happened just before Passover. A group of Greeks had come to Jerusalem to worship at the feast, and they asked for a private audience with Jesus. The news that Jesus had raised Lazarus from the dead had spread quickly and widely. Many had lined the path leading into Jerusalem from the Mount of Olives to shout "Hosanna!" and to declare Jesus as the "King of Israel!" (John 12:12–15). A strong effort was being made to rally support for Jesus to make a public, political move to consolidate power and become an earthly ruler in place of both the Roman occupation and what was perceived by many to be an oppressive, legalistic Jewish Temple rulership.

The Greeks said to Philip, "Sir, we wish to see Jesus." Philip told Andrew of their request, and together, Andrew and Philip went to Jesus. From a human perspective, this could have become a top-level meeting, leading to a human-engineered political coup. Jesus gave this answer: "The hour has come that the Son of Man should be glorified" (John 12:23). On the surface, this statement must have been taken by the disciples and supporters of Jesus to be a strong signal—"Now is the time!" To be glorified means to reach your crowning moment, your shining hour. But then Jesus quickly went on to say this:

> Most assuredly, I say to you, unless a grain of wheat falls into the ground and dies, it remains alone; but if it dies, it produces much grain. He who loves his life will lose it, and he who hates his life in this world will keep it for eternal life. (John 12:24–25)

Jesus made it very clear that He was not called to be a political king so that people might experience a better temporal, earthly existence, but, rather, that He was destined to die a sacrificial death so that man might experience an eternal, spiritual life. Jesus was not called to become a king over a political domain, but, instead, the King of kings who might reign over an eternal kingdom not made with human hands.

The means to achieving Jesus' much higher and more meaningful goal was not to be found in the man-made systems and alliances of this world, but rather through the ultimate act of ministry and servanthood, a sacrificial death.

Jesus followed His statement to Philip and Andrew by saying, "If anyone serves Me, let him follow Me; and where I am, there My servant will be also. If anyone serves Me, him My Father will honor" (John 12:26).

Not only did Jesus choose the servant role for Himself—which was actually the heavenly Father's role for Him—but He called His followers to become like Him, and to be, first and foremost, *servants.*

Jesus concluded, "What shall I say? 'Father, save Me from this hour'? But for this purpose I came to this hour. Father, glorify Your name" (John 12:27). Jesus did not back away from servanthood or the ultimate act of service—His sacrificial death. He did not regard His crucifixion in any way to be a demeaning or diminishing act, but He considered it to be the very purpose for His life and the fulfillment of His time on this earth. His entire life and ministry had been aimed at this supreme act of service.

There's a phrase that embodies this principle: "Make sure that what you are living for is what you are willing to die for." That's the way Jesus lived. He lived a life of service, and He died a death that was an act of service.

•*What new insights do you have into the way Jesus was a servant?*

_____

_____

• *In what ways are you feeling challenged in your spiritual walk with God?*

_____

_____

Poured out Like Water

Psalm 22, which is a prophetic psalm linked very closely to the crucifixion of Jesus, has in it this phrase: "I am poured out like water" (v. 14).

The very life essence of Jesus, indeed, was poured out like water. During His life, He poured Himself out on all those who were hungry and thirsty for the things of God. He gave of Himself freely to all who came to Him in need. He said to a woman by a well in Samaria, "Whoever drinks of the water that I shall give him will never thirst. But the water that I shall give him will become in him a fountain of water springing up into everlasting life" (John 4:14).

In His crucifixion, blood and water mingled freely in flowing from Jesus' side. He willingly gave His life, His blood "poured out" for the sins of the world.

The purpose of being "planted" like a grain of wheat or "poured out" like water is not the sacrificial giving itself, but rather what follows such service: a great blessing and reward. In the case of a grain of wheat being planted, the result is not merely the death of the grain of wheat, but an abundant harvest. The single dying grain produces "much grain" (John 12:24). In pouring Himself out, Jesus intended that His own spirit become a "fountain of water springing up" (John 4:14).

Death or sacrifice in itself is not the goal. Being a servant is not having a martyr's complex—a desire to die just for the sake of dying. Rather, our life is to be poured out in loving and faith-filled service so that what we give bears the quality of life in it. In pouring ourselves out to others, others are quickened to experience greater life, and we, in turn, experience a more purposeful life and ultimately, eternal life. The end result is not a moot death but a glorious everlasting abundance.

It was because servanthood brings about a great blessing that Jesus called His disciples, including you and me, to be servants. He knew that anything you sacrifice in an act of servanthood to God—anything you do as an act of your faith in and love for God—will result in something positive and beneficial to all involved.

Among the many benefits of servanthood are these:

- A radiant excitement in your life for God and for all things that are good
- A healing in your life
- A difference in the lives of those whom you serve
- Inspiration and motivation to those who benefit from and who witness your generous service
- A more fruitful life, both in the natural and supernatural realms

• *Reflect back over times in your life when you knew that you were filling a servant's role for another person. How did you feel? What were the results in your life and the other person's?*

_____

_____

• *Recall a time or experience in which someone acted as a servant to you—meeting a need in your life or helping you in a very specific way. How did you feel? What was the result in your life?*

_____

_____

What the Word Says	What the Word Says to Me
Behold! My Servant whom I have chosen, My Beloved in whom My soul is well pleased! I will put My Spirit upon Him, And He will declare justice to the Gentiles (Matt. 12:18; also Isa. 42:1).	_____ _____ _____ _____ _____ _____
Let this mind be in you which was also in Christ Jesus, who, being in the form of God, did not consider it robbery to be equal with God, but made Himself of no reputation, taking the form of a bondservant, and coming in the likeness of men (Phil. 2:5–7).	_____ _____ _____ _____ _____ _____ _____ _____

Like Master Like Servant

The disciples of Jesus had a very clear understanding of their role as servants. Note how the disciples described themselves:

- "Simon Peter, a bondservant and apostle of Jesus Christ" (2 Peter 1:1)
- "James, a bondservant of God and of the Lord Jesus Christ" (James 1:1)
- "Paul and Timothy, bondservants of Jesus Christ" (Phil. 1:1)
- "Paul, a bondservant of Jesus Christ, called to be an apostle" (Rom. 1:1)
- John wrote at the outset of the book of Revelation, "The Revelation of Jesus Christ, which God gave Him to show His servants—things which must shortly take place." (Rev. 1:1)

The Greek word that is generally translated as "bondservant" in the New Testament is a word that was also used to refer to the "lower rowers"—the galley slaves who were kept in chains below the decks of large ships. They did the exhausting, difficult, and unseen work of rowing vessels across the seas and through the storms. There is absolutely nothing glamorous about being a "lower rower." There is nothing about this image that brings about the praise and admiration of others, since the work goes mostly unrecognized and unrewarded by humankind.

Yet this is the word that the disciples used to describe themselves in their work on behalf of others; they saw it as an honor to be a bondservant of Christ Jesus, a lower rower in the work of God's kingdom.

This concept of success is completely inverted from that of the world's standard. The world tells us, "The successful person is the one at the top, the one who is most visible, most admired, most talented, most accomplished." The Scriptures tell us that in God's eyes, the successful person is the one who is willing, even eager, to be a lower rower for the benefit of others and for the sake of the gospel.

- *How do you imagine it would feel to be a lower rower on a ship in the first century? How does it feel at times to be a lower rower in the kingdom of God?*

_____

_____

The disciples recognized, even as Jesus did, the blessing that came from being a bondservant. They knew that their efforts in the spirit realm were cause for joy because they were helping others to find eternal life in Christ Jesus. Paul wrote to the Philippians from a jail cell, "If I am being poured out as a drink offering on the sacrifice and service of your faith, I am glad and rejoice with you all" (Phil. 2:17).

The disciples fully embraced their role as servants. They knew this to be their calling and identity, *not because they were leaders of the church*, but because they were following in the steps of Jesus Christ, the first and foremost Servant of God.

We are called to be servants today, and to have the heart of a servant as our hallmark, regardless of the area in which we serve the church or the role we fill. Servanthood is to be our attitude and our motivation as we follow Christ Jesus our Lord.

Some people seem to have concluded that it is only pastors or other members of a church staff who are God's servants. In reality, any person who has accepted Jesus Christ as Savior is called to be a servant of God and to be God's minister to others in particular areas of need, at particular times, but *always* with a mind and a heart motivated toward generous service.

What the Word Says	What the Word Says to Me
If anyone serves Me, let him follow Me; and where I am, there My servant will be also (John 12:26).	_____ _____ _____ _____
Through love serve one another (Gal. 5:13).	_____ _____

Nobody is excluded from service. We each are called to serve God and to serve others in need every day of our lives. God has already identified the precise ways in which He desires for you to serve Him and, thereby, fulfill your purpose in life. Ephesians 2:10 tells us:

For we are His workmanship, created in Christ Jesus for good works, which God prepared beforehand that we should walk in them.

Service is the *doing* of good works *as God leads and directs* through the power of the Holy Spirit. The works are there for us to do. Our responsibility is to obey God, even as Jesus obeyed the Father, and to serve Him with *all* of our lives—every last grain, every last bit "poured out" to Him and to others.

• *How is the Lord challenging you to reevaluate your concept of service? In what ways is the Lord challenging you to engage in more active servanthood?*

_____

_____

LESSON 3

A SERVANT'S SPIRIT

The world has a hierarchy, a "ladder," for evaluating the success of a person. Sometimes that ladder is based upon fame, sometimes upon money. In an organization, the person who has made his or her way to the position of CEO or chairman of the board is considered to be at the top of the ladder.

This is not a definition for success that is new to our century or to modern man. Jesus had to deal with this thinking among His own disciples. In fact, even during the Last Supper, a dispute arose among the disciples "as to which of them should be considered the greatest" (Luke 22:24). It wasn't the first time this had happened. Several times in the course of Jesus' ministry we find a concern expressed about position and authority.

Jesus answered His disciples during the Last Supper by saying:

> The kings of the Gentiles exercise lordship over them, and those who exercise authority over them are called "benefactors." But not so among you; on the contrary, he who is greatest among you, let him be as the younger, and he who governs as he who serves. For who is greater [in the world's viewpoint], he who sits at the table, or he who serves? Is it not he who sits at the table? Yet I am among you as the One who serves. (Luke 22:25–27)

This concept of service being equated with greatness seemed completely upside down to the disciples. It was a perspective that went against the grain, against common sense, against the prevailing world opinion. And it still does.

Our world today may regard servants as heroes, but generally only in isolated circumstances and situations.

If a person engages in servanthood all the time, and especially if he or she is a servant at heart in all situations to all people, that person is considered to be a wimp, a chump, a doormat, a nothing, or a nobody. Or, in some cases, such a servant is considered a living saint, but usually by people who don't remotely think sainthood is possible for all people or who believe that service is to become the way of life for all Christians. The person who is widely admired by the masses tends to be the person who has shown himself or herself to have the most power, the most appeal, the most intelligence, the most money, and the most accomplishment—the one at the top of the scale.

God does not deal in hierarchies. He deals only in categories. A person is either saved or unsaved. A person is either following God in obedience or rebelling against God. A person is either a servant or not a servant.

• *Reflect upon your own life experience to date. Can you recall times in which you were a servant? Can you recall times in which you were not a servant?*

_____

_____

A Simple Definition

Jesus gave a very simple definition of service in John 12:25 when He said:

He who loves his life will lose it, and he who hates his life in this world will keep it for eternal life.

The person who loves his life is the person who is self-centered, selfish, greedy—the one who lives totally for his own benefit. This is the person who desires to be *served*. In the end, he will lose everything he has ever attempted to gain for himself.

The person who "hates" his life is the person who is willing to put others first—the one who gives and helps others. This is the person who is a *servant*. In the end, Jesus said, this is the person who will enter into eternal life.

Some people confuse "hating one's life" with having low self-esteem or with diminishing one's gifts. People who are self-deprecating, always saying negative things about themselves, refusing to accept compliments, or who are down on themselves may indeed hate themselves, but this is not what Jesus meant with these words.

We are to value ourselves highly. We are to recognize that we are wonderful, unique creations of God. Each of us has been given a set of gifts, traits, and talents by God. We have been designed with a specific purpose in mind—we *are* God's workmanship (Eph. 2:10). We are God's treasure, His delight, His chosen vessels, His beloved children. The fact is, God valued us so highly that He sent His Son, Jesus Christ, to die on the cross so that we might be reconciled to God and live with Him forever. God's love alone gives our lives great value!

In recognizing our great value to God and in embracing the wonderful qualities that God has placed in us, we have a servant's spirit when we are willing to *use* our gifts for the benefit of others and not solely to bring applause, recognition, or reward to ourselves. We "hate ourselves," from God's standpoint, when we completely abandon our own self-advancement in order to help others in need or to fulfill whatever call of the gospel God has placed upon our lives.

What happens in a very practical way is that those who love their lives tend to hate the lives of other people. They use, abuse, and manipulate others for their own purposes. Those who "hate" their lives are those who, in comparing their own benefit with the good that is to be done for others, choose to love others more than they love their own advancement. They bless, give to, and benefit others.

This is the quality of life that Jesus lived. He didn't dislike Himself or hate the call of God on His life. He knew who He was, and He fully embraced what His heavenly Father had commanded Him to be and to do. But He didn't exalt Himself, seek His own fame and power, or attract attention to Himself. His purpose was to bring glory to the Father and to obey the Father in all things. His purpose was to serve.

Jesus taught, "To whom much is given, from him much will be required" (Luke 12:48).

The more we recognize all that we have been given by God—including God's greatest gift to us, our salvation—the more we should recognize that we are required to give much in the way of service. Those who have the greater talents are required to give the greater service.

Paul wrote to the Philippians that Jesus emptied Himself of His heavenly possessions and identity when He became a bondservant of God and took on the likeness of mankind. He "made Himself of no reputation" (Phil. 2:7). That does not mean that Jesus wasn't worthy or deserving of a good reputation—He had the ultimate reputation in that He never sinned against God or man—but that Jesus was willing to empty Himself of all His gifts and goodness. As one person said, "Jesus gave Himself to death." While some people work themselves to death in order to get ahead in life, it is the person who follows Jesus' example and gives himself to death who receives the great rewards in eternity.

> •*What new insights do you have into God's Word about hating and loving your own life?*

_____

_____

What the Word Says	**What the Word Says to Me**
For everyone to whom much is given, from him much will be required; and to whom much has been committed, of him they will ask the more (Luke 12:48).	
For this is the will of God, that by doing good you may put to silence	

the ignorance of foolish men—as
free, yet not using liberty as a
cloak for vice, but as bondservants
of God (1 Peter 2:15–16).

Three Marks of Servanthood

The person with a genuine servant's heart is a person who bears these attributes:

1. A True Servant Does Not Demand Recognition

A servant is willing to remain in the shadows or the lower galleys. The servant gives without acknowledgment; in fact, he or she is willing to give so that nobody knows who has done the giving.

Jesus had strong words to say about those who behave in certain ways in order to receive the praise of other people. He taught:

> Take heed that you do not do your charitable deeds before men, to be seen by them. Otherwise you have no reward from your Father in heaven. Therefore, when you do a charitable deed, do not sound a trumpet before you as the hypocrites do in the synagogues and in the streets, that they may have glory from men. Assuredly, I say to you, they have their reward. (Matt. 6:1–2)

The reward received by those who seek praise from people is just that and only that—praise from people. Such praise comes and goes very quickly; the approval of people is very fickle and often fleeting. God's praise and blessing are reserved for those who serve others without any expectation of recognition or praise from people.

I am continually amazed at how many people in the body of Christ only want to participate in various aspects of their churches if their names are listed on the committee roster, published in the service bulletin, or engraved on a plaque at the church entrance. I was told recently by a person who works as the development officer for an organization that fewer and fewer projects are named in "honor" of major contributors; the prevailing practice, rather, is to include the naming of a building, hospital wing, or park as a part of the negotiating process for securing the donation in the first place. As Jesus said, those who desire public acclaim have their reward, but it is not an eternal reward granted by God.

What the Word Says	**What the Word Says to Me**
When you do a charitable deed, do not let your left hand know what your right hand is doing, that your charitable deed may be in secret; and your Father who sees in secret will Himself reward you openly (Matt. 6:3–4).	------------------------------- ------------------------------- ------------------------------- ------------------------------- ------------------------------- ------------------------------- -------------------------------
Freely you have received, freely give (Matt. 10:8).	------------------------------- -------------------------------

• *How do you feel when you don't receive recognition for something you have done?*

_____

_____

2. A True Servant Does Not Demand Reward

A servant gives without expecting anything in return from the person he or she has served. True servanthood is void of manipulation or a desire to control others.

The best thing that could happen to a slave or a servant in the ancient world was to have a kind, benevolent, compassionate, and generous master. A servant in such a household knew that all of his needs would be met to the greatest degree possible; such a servant had a sense of security and safety. He or she was not merely the property of the master or "lord," but was considered a valuable asset to be nurtured and rewarded.

Abraham apparently had such servants. We read in Genesis 24:2 that Abraham's oldest servant "ruled over all that he had," and Abraham entrusted him to travel a great distance by himself to find a wife for Isaac, Abraham's son. This servant was faithful to his duty. The thought of escaping to "freedom" with Abraham's ten camels and the considerable wealth entrusted to him was unthinkable.

Joseph was a favored servant in the household of the Egyptian Potiphar, who "left all that he had in Joseph's hand" (Gen. 39:6).

Our role as a bondservant of Christ Jesus is of a similar nature. Jesus Christ is our *Lord*. He is our Master, our Ruler, our Owner. He is the One who has redeemed our lives from death. He is the One from whom we take our daily orders and from whom we receive all that we need. He is the One who has entrusted us to conduct spiritual business in His name.

A genuine servant knows that he or she has, in Christ Jesus, all that he needs, all that is truly important, all that is desirable and of value.

When we give, we *will* receive. But what comes back to us will be from God's hand and at God's command. We are to expect to receive from God *not* because we have given, but because God is faithful in providing for His children, often through supernatural means.

Expecting God to provide for us out of His great storehouse of blessing and His heart of love is far different from *demanding* that God provide for us or reward us because of what we have done. Expecting from God is a mark of faith. Demanding God to act on our behalf is a mark of pride.

What the Word Says	What the Word Says to Me
Do not seek what you should eat or what you should drink, nor have an anxious mind. For all these things the nations of the world seek after, and your Father knows that you need these things (Luke 12:29–30).	-------------------------------
If you do good to those who do good to you, what credit is that to you? For even sinners do the	-------------------------------

same. And if you lend to those
from whom you hope to receive
back, what credit is that to you?
For even sinners lend to sinners to
receive as much back. But love
your enemies, do good, and lend,
hoping for nothing in return; and
your reward will be great, and you
will be sons of the Most High
(Luke 6:33–35).

• *How do you feel when you do not receive a reward from those to whom you give?*

3. A True Servant Does Not Demand Self-Rights

A servant has a "yielded" spirit, both to God and to others. While a servant will stand up for what is right in God's eyes, a person with a genuine servant's heart does not insist that he have his own way. A servant "yields the right of way" to others, or as Paul wrote, "giving preference to one another" (Rom. 12:10).

The hallmark of the Christian life is reflected in Ephesians 5:20–21:

Giving thanks always for all things to God the Father in the name of our Lord Jesus Christ, submitting to one another in the fear of God.

We are to love God with all of our heart, soul, and mind, and our neighbors as ourselves. It is out of love that we *serve*. In fact, service is the manifestation of love. If you love, but you do not give to a person and are not generous in your service to that person, on what grounds can you truly say that you love? Service is the evidence of genuine love. It is love in action.

What the Word Says	**What the Word Says to Me**
[Love] does not behave rudely, does not seek its own (1 Cor. 13:5).	_____ _____ _____
Be kindly affectionate to one another with brotherly love, in honor giving preference to one another (Rom. 12:10).	_____ _____ _____ _____
Jesus said to him, 'You shall love the LORD your God with all your heart, with all your soul, and with all your mind.' This is the first and great commandment. And the second is like it: 'You shall love your neighbor as yourself' (Matt. 22:37–39).	_____ _____ _____ _____ _____ _____ _____ _____

• *How do you feel when your rights seem to be ignored or trampled upon?*

_____

_____

•*What new insights do you have into the nature of service—and how difficult it can be to truly have a servant's heart?*

_____

_____

A Serious Challenge

If most of us were asked, "Are you God's servant?" we would probably respond, "Yes, I am. He is my King; I am His subject. Jesus Christ is my Lord. I am His servant."

The more difficult questions to answer, however, are these: "Do you truly have a servant's heart? Are you not only willing to serve, but are you presently serving others without demanding recognition, rewards, or 'rights'?"

Many people only give lip service to servanthood. They say they are servants, want to be servants, or wish they were better servants. The truth is, we can all grow in our desire, ability, and effectiveness as servants. We must, however, actually *be* servants—not just talk about being servants. James said:

> Be doers of the word, and not hearers only, deceiving yourselves. For if anyone is a hearer of the word and not a doer, he is like a man observing his natural face in a mirror; for he observes himself, goes away, and immediately forgets what kind of man he was. But he who looks into the perfect law of liberty and continues in it, and is not a forgetful hearer but a doer of the work, this one will be blessed in what he does. (James 1:22–25)

The true servant is not only one who has a heart for service or a desire to be a better servant, but one who is actually engaged in serving.

• *In what ways do you feel challenged in your walk with the Lord?*

_____

_____

LESSON 4

JESUS: OUR ROLE MODEL AS SERVANT

One of the names given to Jesus in the New Testament is "Son of David." For many people, this title evokes the kingship of Jesus—and rightfully so. David was a great king, and Jesus is our King of kings.

In Acts 13:36 we read, however, this perspective on the life of King David from the apostle Paul: "For David, after he had served his own generation by the will of God." David was not regarded by the first disciples of Jesus primarily as a great soldier, statesman, king, or psalmist—although he certainly filled all of those role—abut as a *servant*. David was perceived as being used by God for God's purposes. He functioned as a servant of God to the people of Israel. Servanthood under God's command and authority was David's most important trait.

In this way, Jesus is most assuredly like David. He was and is the supreme Servant.

Both David and Jesus knew the secret for true success from God's perspective: *Discover God's goals for your life and then achieve those goals.*

God's goals for David were that he unify God's people into one nation, create a centralized place for the worship of God, place a renewed emphasis upon praise before God, and defeat the enemies of God. In fulfilling these goals, David *served*.

God's goal in sending Jesus to this earth was that Jesus might show us what God is like, through both word and deed, revealing to us a loving, healing, saving, and delivering heavenly Father. God's goal was also that Jesus might become the definitive and universal sacrifice for the sins of all mankind. In fulfilling these goals, Jesus *served*.

> • *Reflect upon your own life. What goals do you believe God has for you? How is the fulfilling of those goals your means of serving God?*

A Life of Service

We often think of Jesus' ministry, or His years of "active service," as being the final three years of His life on earth. What we often fail to recognize is that for nearly thirty years, Jesus *served* His family. The historical tradition within the Christian church is that Joseph, Jesus' earthly father, died when Jesus was a young man, perhaps even a young teenager. As the eldest son in the family, Jesus became responsible for the general well-being of His mother and His earthly brothers and sisters. In all likelihood, Jesus filled this role in a very practical way—providing the family income and helping in the training of his younger siblings—until the youngest of His siblings was either married or had reached adulthood.

You may feel that your life right now is so busy with family obligations and responsibilities that you cannot serve God. The truth is, you are serving God as you serve your family. That may be the sole or primary role that God has for you right now. Be a parent as if you were a parent to the Lord Jesus Himself. When you serve your children from that perspective and with that motivation, you are serving God.

It was in serving His family that Jesus no doubt developed a great deal of the compassion we see in Him during His ministry years:

He reached out to children, He touched lepers, He embraced outcasts, He quieted the fears of the fearful. Compassion is a trait that is part of Jesus' *humanity* as much as His divinity. One does not develop overnight this ability to care for others; it was a pattern that had grown in Jesus throughout His years of caring for His own family.

> • *How do you feel about the service you give your family, and about how Jesus cared for His family? In what ways do you feel challenged in your spirit?*

_____

_____

A Profound Act of Service

One of the most profound acts of service in Jesus' life occurred during the Last Supper that He shared with His disciples before the Crucifixion. As you read through these verses, mark those words and phrases that stand out in a special way to you.

And supper being ended, the devil having already put it into the heart of Judas Iscariot, Simon's son, to betray Him, Jesus, knowing that the Father had given all things into His hands, and that He had come from God and was going to God, rose from supper and laid aside His garments, took a towel and girded Himself. After that, He poured water into a basin and began to wash the disciples' feet, and to wipe them with the towel with which He was girded. Then He came to Simon Peter. And Peter said to Him, "Lord, are You washing my feet?"

Jesus answered and said to him, "What I am doing you do not understand now, but you will know after this."

Peter said to Him, "You shall never wash my feet!"

Jesus answered him, "If I do not wash you, you have no part with Me."

pressure

Passion

Peace c proceed use

Simon Peter said to Him, "Lord, not my feet only, but also my hands and my head!"

Jesus said to him, "He who is bathed needs only to wash his feet, but is completely clean; and you are clean, but not all of you." For He knew who would betray Him; therefore He said, "You are not all clean."

So when He had washed their feet, taken His garments, and sat down again, He said to them, "Do you know what I have done to you? You call Me Teacher and Lord, and you say well, for so I am. If I then, your Lord and Teacher, have washed your feet, you also ought to wash one another's feet. For I have given you an example, that you should do as I have done to you. Most assuredly, I say to you, a servant is not greater than his master; nor is he who is sent greater than he who sent him. If you know these things, blessed are you if you do them." (John 13:2–17)

•*What new insights do you have into this passage of Scripture?*

_____

_____

Some churches have turned foot washing into a frequent ceremony. While I don't necessarily disagree with that practice, I certainly do not believe that Jesus established foot washing as an *ordinance* for the church—something that we must do in a scheduled ceremonial fashion. Jesus said He was giving us an example. A foot-washing ceremony can be very meaningful, but it is meaningful only to the extent that it is an *example* of humility in service one to another.

What Jesus was most concerned about in washing the feet of His disciples was that they see demonstrated an attitude and a character of ministry that were important for them to have. Jesus used a vivid means of demonstration so that His disciples would never forget His principal truth to them: You must be the servants of one another.

We know from another of the Gospel accounts (Luke 22:24) that the disciples were disputing at the Last Supper which of them was to be considered the greatest. Jesus' response to this dispute was an act of service.

Normally, the host of a home would provide servants to wash the feet of guests as they entered the house from the dusty streets of the city and roads of the countryside. Guests were expected to come to banquets or dinners such as the one that became Jesus' Last Supper, having bathed and wearing clean garments. This is what Jesus meant, in part, when He said, "You are already bathed; now you are fully clean."

His meaning went deeper, however. Jesus was referring to their spiritual nature. Jesus went on to explain during the Last Supper: "You are already clean because of the word which I have spoken to you. Abide in Me, and I in you" (John 15:3–4). He knew that all but one of the disciples, Judas, had fully believed the words of Jesus and were abiding in Him. Judas, however, had chosen to harbor rebellion in his heart and was *not* abiding fully in the words of Jesus.

Why did Peter initially balk at having Jesus wash his feet? One of the reasons no doubt was because Peter was sitting at the "foot" of the table. In occupying that position during the supper, it was his responsibility to be the servant of the table if there was no other servant. If feet had needed washing, it should have been Peter who was doing the foot washing. Peter certainly must have felt embarrassed that Jesus was preparing to do what Peter should have done.

Jesus insisted on washing Peter's feet, however, against Peter's protests. He wanted Peter to see very clearly that unless Peter learned to receive from Jesus all that Jesus desired to do for him—including the greatest service of all yet to come, His sacrificial death on the cross—Peter would not be in a position to serve others. It is only as we receive service, or ministry, from Jesus that we can become true servants to others.

The lesson to Peter and the other disciples was this: *As* Jesus served them, so they were to serve others. They were to be just as sensitive as Jesus to the needs of others, just as responsive as Jesus to the needs they perceived, and just as generous as Jesus in their loving care of others.

The same is true for us. We are to serve others in humility and kindness, just as Jesus washed the dusty feet of His disciples only hours before His arrest and crucifixion.

What the Word Says	What the Word Says to Me
Whom He foreknew, He also predestined to be conformed to the image of His Son, that He might be the firstborn among many brethren (Rom. 8:29).	-------------------
A servant is not greater than his master; nor is he who is sent greater than he who sent him. If you know these things, blessed are you if you do them (John 13:16–17).	-------------------

Service to the Least Deserving

One of the things I want you to notice in the example of Jesus washing the feet of His disciples is this: Jesus washed the feet of Judas. He knelt before the man who already had aligned himself with Jesus' enemies and who would betray Him within a matter of hours in the Garden of Gethsemane. Jesus *knew* what He was doing even as He washed the feet of Judas. He said, "I know whom I have chosen" (John 13:18).

Many people find it easy to serve those who are good people—perhaps those who seem temporarily down on their luck or are going through a crisis or transition that has left them in need. It is much more difficult for most people to serve with generosity and fervor those whom we consider to be "bad." It is much harder to take a basin and towel and to kneel before a mean-spirited, deliberately rebellious, or hardened person. Jesus, however, is our example. He washed the feet of the man who was the ultimate hypocrite, pleasant to His face, but 99 percent opposed to Him in his heart.

• *Have you ever been required to serve someone who was unlovable or difficult to please? How did you feel about your service?*

_____

_____

• *Have you ever been the benefactor of service from someone even though you knew that you were acting in a less-than-Christlike manner? How did you feel about that person's service to you?*

_____

_____

Paul had specific words to say to those who found it difficult to serve their masters. A number of people who became part of the first-century church were slaves—some to Christian masters and some to unbelievers. These slaves, free in their spirits in Christ Jesus, nonetheless were called to continue to be servants. These Christian believers were richly blessed and endowed with spiritual gifts, yet they were required to continue to do the most demeaning and humbling acts of service in the practical realm. As you read the passages of Scripture below, apply what Paul and Peter wrote to *your* service of others.

What the Word Says	What the Word Says to Me
Let as many bondservants as are under the yoke count their own masters worthy of all honor, so that the name of God and His doctrine may not be blasphemed. And those who have believing masters, let them not despise them because they are brethren, but rather serve them because those who are benefited are believers and beloved (1 Tim. 6:1–2).	---------------------------------- ---------------------------------- ---------------------------------- ---------------------------------- ---------------------------------- ---------------------------------- ---------------------------------- ---------------------------------- ---------------------------------- ---------------------------------- ----------------------------------
Servants, be submissive to your	----------------------------------

masters with all fear, not only to
the good and gentle, but also to
the harsh. For this is commendable, if because of conscience
toward God one endures grief,
suffering wrongfully. For what
credit is it if, when you are beaten
for your faults, you take it
patiently? But when you do good
and suffer, if you take it patiently,
this is commendable before God.
For to this you were called,
because Christ also suffered for
us, leaving us an example, that
you should follow His steps
(1 Peter 2:18–21).

_____
_____
_____
_____
_____
_____
_____
_____
_____
_____
_____
_____
_____
_____
_____
_____

•*What new insights do you have into servanthood?*

_____

_____

The Most Menial of Tasks

In washing the feet of His disciples, Jesus was engaging in one of the most menial tasks that a household servant performed in the first century. Jesus was sending a clear message that He was will-ing to do *anything* for His disciples.

Are you willing to do *anything* that God asks of you today? God will never ask you to do anything that is sinful or that is foolish. Neither act would bring glory to His name. But God may ask you to do something that is extremely menial.

In my years as a pastor (prior to teaching this series of lessons) I never once had a person come to me and say, "Pastor, give me the most menial job in the church. Give me the chore that is the worst to do or the job that is least likely to be recognized." If such a person had come to me, I certainly would have felt that I was in the presence of genuine greatness.

If you are too good for a task, the reality is that you probably are not good enough for it in God's eyes. Any job done "as unto the Lord" is a worthy one, regardless of the nature of the job or the degree of recognition that is associated with it. Keep in mind always that the world's idea of success and service is not God's idea for success and service within His kingdom.

Is there anybody whose feet you would refuse to wash? That may very well be the person whom God most desires for you to serve!

What the Word Says	What the Word Says to Me
He who is greatest among you shall be your servant (Matt. 23:11).	_____ _____ _____
Jesus called a little child to Him, set him in the midst of them, and said, "Assuredly, I say to you, unless you are converted and become as little children, you will by no means enter the kingdom of heaven. Therefore whoever humbles himself as this little child is the greatest in the kingdom of heaven" (Matt. 18:2–4).	_____ _____ _____ _____ _____ _____ _____ _____ _____ _____

Serving "As Unto the Lord"

The disciples learned the lesson that Jesus sought to teach them. From the time of Jesus' crucifixion and resurrection onward, they equated all forms of service to others as means of serving Jesus. Jesus had taught them this lesson about service not only in His washing the disciples' feet, but in His receiving a special gift from Mary of Bethany. We read in the Gospel of John:

Six days before the Passover, Jesus came to Bethany, where Lazarus was who had been dead, whom He had raised from the dead. There they made Him a supper; and Martha served, but Lazarus was one of those who sat at the table with Him. Then Mary took a pound of very costly oil of spikenard, anointed the feet of Jesus, and wiped His feet with her hair. And the house was filled with the fragrance of the oil . . . . Jesus said, . . . "She has kept this for the day of My burial." (John 12:1–3, 7)

Jesus not only knew how to give service to His disciples in washing their feet, but He knew how to *receive* the service of those who loved and followed Him. He allowed Mary to anoint His feet and to demonstrate her love in this way. Her giving was a sign of Jesus' impending death.

When we serve others today, we ultimately are serving Jesus. We are demonstrating our love for Him in the way we minister to others. Our gifts to Jesus, through our service to those around us, are also a sign—a sign of His resurrection power and His desire to save and heal all humankind. Our service is the greatest witness we can give to the Lord Jesus.

An act of service is *anything* we do that promotes the kingdom of God, especially those things that are clearly characterized as being righteous, peaceful, and joyous (Rom. 14:17–18).

• *How do you feel about serving Christ by serving others?*

_____

_____

• *In what ways are you feeling challenged in your spirit?*

_____

_____

What the Word Says

Bondservants, obey in all things your masters according to the flesh, not with eyeservice, as men-pleasers, but in sincerity of heart, fearing God. And whatever you do, do it heartily, as to the Lord and not to men, knowing that

What the Word Says to Me

----

from the Lord you will receive the
reward of the inheritance; for you
serve the Lord Christ (Col.
3:22–24).

The kingdom of God is not eating
and drinking, but righteousness
and peace and joy in the Holy
Spirit. For he who serves Christ in
these things is acceptable to God
and approved by men (Rom.
14:17–18).

The Greatest Service of All

The ultimate service of Jesus can be summed up in one word: Cross. As I indicated at the outset of this lesson, God's goal for Jesus was that He become the sacrifice for our sin. Jesus fulfilled that goal in His death on the cross.

God doesn't let any person get by with sin. Sin causes us to be estranged from God, and God's purpose is always to reach out to us and bring us to reconciliation with Himself. He continues to convict us of our sin until we come to a point of confession. After we have received God's gift of forgiveness, if we fall into sin and error, the Holy Spirit convicts us until we confess, and by His power, repent and live in righteousness before Him.

The soul that sins willfully and continually, ultimately dies (Acts 3:23). Jesus was God's supreme means of atonement—of bringing God and man into relationship so that man might be free of guilt and eternal death. It is for this purpose of atonement that Jesus came into this world.

A significant part of God's purpose for your life is that you be a witness to God's love through all that you do and say. You are to be a witness to God's saving power. While you are not required by God to die on the cross, you are called by God to live and die in such a way that others are made increasingly aware of God's plan of forgiveness.

Service cannot be separated from witness or ministry. When you serve others with joy, peace, and righteousness radiating from you, you are a witness to God's love and desire to forgive, a witness to Christ's crucifixion and resurrection, and a witness to the Holy Spirit's empowering and guiding presence. When you serve others, you *are* a minister . . . you are embodying the work of the Holy Spirit to others.

Can you have a witness without service? Can you truly minister to others without having a servant's heart? You may give a *form* of witness or ministry, but you will not be a genuine witness, and your ministry will not bear much fruit unless you have a servant's heart and are motivated by your love for Christ Jesus.

What the Word Says	What the Word Says to Me
For the grace of God that brings salvation has appeared to all men, teaching us that, denying ungodliness and worldly lusts, we should live soberly, righteously, and godly in the present age, looking for the blessed hope and glorious appearing of our great God and Savior Jesus Christ, who gave Himself for us, that He might redeem us from every lawless deed and purify for Himself His own special people, zealous for good works (Titus 2:11–14).	----------------------------------
He Himself is the propitiation for our sins, and not for ours only but also for the whole world (1 John 2:2).	----------------------------------
Whoever desires to come after Me, let him deny himself, and take up his cross, and follow Me (Mark 8:34).	----------------------------------

• *What new insights do you have into what it means to have a servant's heart?*

_____

_____

• *In what ways are you feeling challenged in your spirit?*

_____

_____

LESSON 5

THE PATTERN FOR SERVICE

S ervice nearly always follows a very specific sequence, one embodied in the life and ministry of Jesus Christ. A prime example of this sequence is in the way Jesus dealt with Zacchaeus, a tax collector in Jericho.

At the time Jesus met Zacchaeus, He was on His way to Jerusalem for the last time. He was probably less than two weeks away from His death on the cross, which Jesus knew would happen during the upcoming Passover Feast. Jericho is one of the well-known cities that Jesus passed through as He left the Galilee area and made His way south to Jerusalem.

Luke 19:1–10 gives us the story that is the theme for this lesson:

> Then Jesus entered and passed through Jericho. Now behold, there was a man named Zacchaeus who was a chief tax collector, and he was rich. And he sought to see who Jesus was, but could not because of the crowd, for he was of short stature. So he ran ahead and climbed up into a sycamore tree to see Him, for He was going to pass that way. And when Jesus came to the place, He looked up and saw him, and said to him, "Zacchaeus, make haste and come down, for today I must stay at your house." So he made haste and came down, and received Him joyfully. But when they saw it, they all complained, saying, "He has gone to be a guest with a man who is a sinner."

Then Zacchaeus stood and said to the Lord, "Look, Lord, I give half of my goods to the poor; and if I have taken anything from anyone by false accusation, I restore fourfold."

And Jesus said to him, "Today salvation has come to this house, because he also is a son of Abraham; for the Son of Man has come to seek and to save that which was lost."

The sequence or pattern of service is fivefold: awareness, availability, acceptance, abiding, and abandonment. Read through the story about Jesus and Zacchaeus again and circle words and phrases that seem to relate to these terms.

Step #1: Awareness

Zacchaeus was a lonely, wealthy, hopeful, desperate man. Luke tells us that he was short in stature, which explains why he climbed up into a sycamore tree. But Jesus did not single out Zacchaeus because he was short, or because he was in a tree. Jesus responded to Zacchaeus because He saw in him a need, a desire, a longing.

Zacchaeus was the chief tax collector in Jericho. In this position, he worked for Rome. Zacchaeus, therefore, was considered by his fellow Jews to be part of the evil oppression that had been placed upon the Jewish people by the Roman occupation forces. Tax collectors working for Rome often collected more than the tax due, and they often became very wealthy in the process of cheating others. Tax collectors were much despised and were considered to be great sinners.

When the crowds saw Zacchaeus attempting to get close enough to see Jesus, it was no wonder that the crowd "closed ranks" and did not let him through.

John said about Jesus that He "knew all men, and had no need that anyone should testify of man, for He knew what was in man" (John 2:24–25). We find evidence of this a number of times in the Gospels when we read that Jesus knew the hearts of men or that He knew what people were thinking and attempting to do. Jesus *knew* Zacchaeus even though they had never met. He did not see him as a short man, a rich man, or a tax collector. He saw him as a man desperate for grace and the good news that God might forgive his sins, reconcile him fully to Himself, and restore him to his people.

• *In your experience, have you ever discovered that someone was not on the inside who you thought that person to be on the basis of what you had observed on the outside?*

_____

_____

• *Have you ever been misjudged in your life as being something that you aren't on the basis of your appearance or outward demeanor?*

_____

_____

Awareness is the first step toward service. If you don't see people as Jesus sees them, you cannot minister to them as Jesus did. Before you can reach out to help someone, you must first see that person as having a need.

Many people are so totally turned inward that they don't see others or hear their inner moanings and weepings. The fact is, every person I know is in need in some area of his or her life. We all have problems, concerns, worries, struggles, temptations, and sorrows that nobody knows about and that we often try to keep hidden.

One of the greatest stories in the Bible about awareness is found in Luke 8:42–48:

> But as He went, the multitudes thronged him. Now a woman, having a flow of blood for twelve years, who had spent all her livelihood on physicians and could not be healed by any, came from behind and touched the border of His garment. And immediately her flow of blood stopped.
>
> And Jesus said, "Who touched Me?"

When all denied it, Peter and those with him said, "Master, the multitudes throng and press You, and You say, 'Who touched Me?'"

But Jesus said, "Somebody touched Me, for I perceived power going out from Me." Now when the woman saw that she was not hidden, she came trembling; and falling down before Him, she declared to Him in the presence of all the people the reason she had touched Him and how she was healed immediately.

And He said to her, "Daughter, be of good cheer; your faith has made you well. Go in peace."

• *What new insights do you have into this passage from the Bible?*

He was aware of her in the crowd

You and I are called to become so sensitive to the needs of others that we *know* when someone is in need of healing and when they are reaching out to Jesus, even though they may not initially confess to their need. We are to serve those in need with confidence and with confidentiality. Our sensitive service to them can cause them to touch Jesus with renewed faith and bring them to a place of healing.

• *In what ways are you feeling challenged in your spiritual walk?*

To be Others Centered

Step #2: Availability

God is never too busy to hear the prayers of His people. Jesus was never too busy to respond to those who sought His help.

When Jesus healed the woman who had had a flow of blood for twelve years, He was on His way to the home of a synagogue ruler, Jairus. Jairus's little girl had become extremely ill and was thought to be on her deathbed. Even so, Jesus stopped to complete the healing in someone who had reached out to Him with her faith. He had *time* for her.

When Jesus encountered Zacchaeus in Jericho, Jesus was on His way to a final week of ministry in Jerusalem—a week that would culminate in His death on the cross and resurrection from the grave. Nothing was more important in the overall life of Jesus than His sacrificial death and resurrection from the dead. And yet, He had *time* for Zacchaeus.

The woman with an unstoppable hemorrhage was considered to be unclean, an outcast in society. According to the religious Jews, this woman had no right to be in a crowd of people or to touch anyone, much less Jesus.

Zacchaeus was a hated tax collector, a sinner in the eyes of all who lived in Jericho. He, too, was a social outcast.

And yet, Jesus made Himself available both to the hemorrhaging woman and the despised tax collector.

People today are starving for the gifts of time and concern. They are desperate for someone to listen to them or to pay attention to them. Sometimes those who need our time and attention the most are those who are held in very low esteem by society. Homeless shelters, prisons, nursing homes, and hospitals for the mentally ill are filled with people who are lonely and forsaken, outcasts.

On virtually every block in every neighborhood of our nation one can find a person who is in need of a friend who will simply listen with heartfelt concern. It may be an older person, perhaps one who has recently lost a spouse. It may be a young mother who stays home alone all day with young children. It may be a sick person or someone who has retired or lost a job.

We must be available to people in need if we are to serve them as Jesus served.

What the Word Says

What the Word Says to Me

Then the righteous will answer Him, saying, "Lord, when did we see You hungry and feed You, or

_____

_____

_____

thirsty and give You drink? When
did we see You a stranger and take
You in, or naked and clothe You?
Or when did we see You sick, or in
prison, and come to You?" And
the King will answer and say to
them, "Assuredly, I say to you,
inasmuch as you did it to one of
the least of these My brethren,
you did it to Me" (Matt.
25:37–40).

Let no one seek his own, but each
one the other's well-being (1 Cor.
10:24).

Step #3: Acceptance

Jesus did not say to Zacchaeus, "Clean up your act. When you
stop collecting taxes, I'll come to your house." He didn't say to the
woman with a flow of blood, "As soon as you stop bleeding, come
see Me."

No! Jesus accepted both Zacchaeus and this woman just as they
were.

Accepting others does not mean that we accept the way they are
without an intent of helping change things for the better. It means
accepting them where they are in order that we might help them
move forward in their lives. Jesus did not leave Zacchaeus the same
way He found him. As the result of Jesus' going to Zacchaeus's
house, Zacchaeus had a change of heart. In His encounter with the
woman who was hemorrhaging, Jesus not only healed her body
but restored her to her community—He made her *whole*.

Our motivation must always be to serve people in Christ, to help
them to become all they can be as God's children. Acceptance is
neither a denial of their current condition nor is it a belief that
things can never improve for the person.

We err greatly if we require others to "get good" before we help
them "get God." God did not place any preconditions upon us before
He forgave us generously. We therefore are in no position to place pre-

conditions upon others. We must accept them as they are and serve them just as we would serve the most righteous and highly esteemed person we know. This is the very essence of unconditional love.

• *How does it feel to be unconditionally loved and fully accepted by another person? How do you seek to respond to someone who loves and accepts you fully just as you are?*

Secure - / Joyful / Promising / Hopeful / Productive

What the Word Says	What the Word Says to Me
Heal the sick, cleanse the lepers, raise the dead, cast out demons. Freely you have received, freely give (Matt. 10:8).	
This is My commandment, that you love one another as I have loved you. Greater love has no one than this, than to lay down one's life for his friends (John 15:12–13).	
Let love be without hypocrisy. . . . Be kindly affectionate to one another with brotherly love, in honor giving preference to one another; not lagging in diligence, fervent in spirit, serving the Lord; rejoicing in hope, patient in tribulation, continuing steadfastly in prayer; distributing to the needs of the saints, given to hospitality (Rom. 12:9–13).	

Step #4: Abiding

The Scriptures say that Jesus "stayed" at the house of Zacchaeus. He was there long enough for a meal, perhaps even an overnight stay.

To serve others best, we must "abide" with them. We must walk in their shoes, see things through their eyes, be close enough to them and spend enough time with them to truly be of lasting benefit to them. Service is not a "hit-and-run" activity.

Jesus made earth His abode for about thirty years. God did not send His Son to deliver a quick thirty-second message from a cloud in the sky. He sent Him to live among men and abide with them day in and day out, through all kinds of circumstances and situations, so that they might truly see Him and know Him fully.

We are called to abide in Christ always—to be in such close relationship with Him and His Word that it is virtually impossible for others to tell where our thoughts end and His begin, or where our love ends and His begins (John 8:31–32; 15:5).

At the same time, we are to abide in loving relationship with others; we are to be the "body" of Christ. It is only when we serve others in this way that people can count on us to be there in a time of need. When we abide with others and *remain* available to them, over a period of time and in various situations, our witness becomes truly strong and steadfast to them. When we are in abiding relationships, we draw closer together in God's love.

The person who flits from ministry to ministry, church to church, job to job, or outreach to outreach is far less effective than the person who puts down roots and chooses to *abide* in relationship with others.

> • *In your experience, recall someone whom you believe has chosen to abide with you in steadfast friendship. How does it feel to have that kind of friend? In what ways do you serve one another?*

_____

_____

One of the best examples in the Scriptures of abiding is in the early church. When believers in Christ were ostracized by their families and friends, they banded together. Many of the new Christians lost their jobs, their inheritances, or their social standing. Rather than turn away from Christ, however, they turned toward Christ and toward one another, helping one another in very practical ways and forming a community of *service* that resulted in adequate provision for all (Acts 2:44–47). The result was a continuing revival. As people saw how the new Christians loved and cared for one another, they were drawn to Christ as never before.

What was true then is true today. When unbelievers see Christians loving and serving one another, and also reaching out to others in need, they say, "I want to be a part of that group. I want what those people have."

What the Word Says	What the Word Says to Me
Behold, how good and how pleasant it is For brethren to dwell together in unity! It is like the precious oil upon the head, . . . For there the Lord commanded the blessing— Life forevermore (Ps. 133:1–3).	---------------------------- ---------------------------- ---------------------------- ---------------------------- ---------------------------- ---------------------------- ---------------------------- ---------------------------- ---------------------------- ----------------------------
Now all who believed were together, and had all things in common, and sold their possessions and goods, and divided them among all, as anyone had need. So continuing daily with one accord in the temple, and breaking bread from house to house, they ate their food with gladness and simplicity of heart, praising God and having favor with all the people. And the Lord added to the church daily those who were being saved (Acts 2:44–47).	---------------------------- ---------------------------- ---------------------------- ---------------------------- ---------------------------- ---------------------------- ---------------------------- ---------------------------- ---------------------------- ---------------------------- ---------------------------- ---------------------------- ---------------------------- ----------------------------

Step #5: Abandonment

The ultimate step in service is self-abandonment—laying aside all of one's selfish desires and all of one's personal agenda in order to do whatever God asks.

When Mary of Bethany broke her bottle of very costly oil of spikenard and poured it over Jesus' feet, she engaged in an act of self-abandonment. Nothing mattered to her but serving Jesus.

When Jesus entered the home of Zacchaeus, He abandoned any concern for His public reputation. He knew the majority of the people in Jericho would accuse Him of aligning with a sinner. He was willing to risk a loss of general public esteem in order to bring salvation to the household of Zacchaeus.

When Peter went to the house of Cornelius, he abandoned years of prejudice against Gentiles. He was willing to go because it was clear to him that God was calling him to go, even if it meant stepping outside the bounds of his own "comfort zone" (Acts 10).

When four men carried their paralyzed friend to Jesus on a stretcher and tore a hole in the roof in order to lower him into Jesus' presence when they couldn't get past the crowd in the doorway, they abandoned their own schedule, their own desires, and what many would have said was their common sense. They let nothing stand in the way of helping their friend get to Jesus (Mark 2:1–12).

God calls us to abandon our concern for ourselves and to move outside ourselves in service to others. In so doing, we actually find ourselves and enter into the true meaning for our lives.

Self-abandonment was the message that Jesus had for a rich young man who came to Him one day and asked, "Good Teacher, what shall I do that I may inherit eternal life?" Jesus reminded him of the commandments, which this man not only knew but had kept diligently. Being a good, religious man, however, was not enough. Jesus called him to a degree of abandonment in service. He said, "One thing you lack: Go your way, sell whatever you have and give to the poor, and you will have treasure in heaven; and come, take up the cross, and follow Me" (Mark 10:21). Utter and complete abandonment to self and self-interests is what Jesus required of this young man—it is also what He requires of us.

• *Have you had an experience in your life in which you abandoned all concern of self to help another person? How did you feel? What were the results?*

_____

_____

• *Have you had an experience in which you knew another person was abandoning his or her self-interests to help you? How did you feel? What was your response?*

_____

_____

What the Word Says	What the Word Says to Me
Jesus answered and said, "Assuredly, I say to you, there is no one who has left house or brothers or sisters or father or mother or wife or children or lands, for My sake and the gospel's, who shall not receive a hundredfold now in this time— houses and brothers and sisters and mothers and children and lands, with persecutions—and in the age to come, eternal life. But many who are first will be last, and the last first" (Mark 10:29–31).	_____ _____ _____ _____ _____ _____ _____ _____ _____ _____ _____ _____ _____ _____
I will show you my faith by my works (James 2:18).	_____ _____

Where Are You in Your Service?

Once again, the pattern toward full service is this: awareness, availability, acceptance, abiding, and abandonment. Where are you in your service? To what next step is God calling you?

You must be aware of the needs of others before you will ever make an effort to meet those needs. You must be available if you are to serve. You must accept others fully, just as they are, if you are to give them the unconditional love of Christ. It is as you abide with others in fellowship over time that your service becomes steadfast and reliable, and your heart is knit to the hearts of others whom you are serving and from whom you are receiving service. Finally, the servant is called to complete abandonment—not merely serving others some of the time, but living in a constant state of outreach to others at all times—on the job, at home, in the community, at church, and wherever God leads.

• *What new insights do you have into what it means to have a servant's heart?*

_____

_____

• *In what ways is God challenging you today?*

_____

_____

THE QUALITIES OF AN EFFECTIVE SERVANT: PART 1

Early in the life of the church, we find a portrait of effective service, which is, in its most basic form, service that meets the very real needs, both material and spiritual, of God's people.

The church grew rapidly after the ascension of Jesus, both in the strict Orthodox community and the Greek-influenced community of Jews in Jerusalem. The Hellenists (Greek-influenced) began to complain that the widows of the Hebrews (Orthodox) were being shown favoritism at the communal meals held daily by the church. The twelve apostles called a meeting of a large number of the Christian disciples in the city and said this:

> It is not desirable that we should leave the word of God and serve tables. Therefore, brethren, seek out from among you seven men of good reputation, full of the Holy Spirit and wisdom, whom we may appoint over this business; but we will give ourselves continually to prayer and to the ministry of the word. (Acts 6:2–4)

This decision pleased the entire group and they chose seven men:

> Stephen, a man full of faith and the Holy Spirit, and Philip, Prochorus, Nicanor, Timon, Parmenas, and Nicolas, a proselyte from Antioch, whom they set before the apostles; and when they had prayed, they laid hands on them. (Acts 6:5–6)

Deacons

These seven men were commissioned for a very specific role in the church. It was not the same role as that of the apostles, but it nevertheless was a vital *ministry* role within the church. These seven men became the first deacons.

The word for *deacon* in the Greek language, *diakonos*, had a much different meaning from the meaning of the word today in most Christian denominations. In many of our churches today, deacons are chosen for their business ability, their intelligence, their position in the world, and their income level. Once elected as deacons, they often attempt to fill spiritual roles of leadership.

The first deacons, however, represent an almost 180-degree difference in role. They were chosen for spiritual qualities, not "professional" qualities, and once appointed, they then were given very practical roles of service. They were not rulers, per se.

The word *diakonos* is also used in the Greek language to literally express the concepts "to run, to hasten." The first deacons were expected to be quick in their response to meeting the needs they perceived among the growing body of Christian believers. They were given the job of protecting the harmony of the fellowship—of making sure that things were done equitably and in order, of making certain that all the needs were met, and of ensuring that no clique groups developed within the body of Christ.

The first deacons were chosen on the basis of six qualities in their lives: They were submissive, of good reputation, full of the Holy Spirit, and they had wisdom, vision for the work of God, and humility. These are the same qualities that today make for the most effective servants.

•*What new insights do you have into God's Word and to the importance of service in the church?*

_____

_____

The Quality of Submissiveness

The deacons were under the authority of apostles. The apostles were the ones who laid hands upon the deacons, prayed for them, and imparted to them their authority within the church. In many churches today, this process has been turned upside down—the deacons are the ones who call the pastors and then lay hands on them and commission them to serve their local church. The original order established in the first-century church is not only far more effective, but it is *God's* design.

The apostles were the ones who devoted themselves to prayer and the ministry of the Word. They were the ones who preached the gospel of Jesus to those who were not yet a part of the fellowship of Christians, and they no doubt were the ones who baptized the new converts upon their acceptance of Christ. *Apostle* literally means "one sent out," and the apostles filled this role—they were at the cutting edge of the outreach of the church.

The role of the deacons was turned inward toward the believers. The deacons were responsible for running the practical matters in the church. While they certainly were men of prayer and were no doubt students of God's Word, prayer and preaching were not their primary responsibilities.

This does not mean that on occasion a deacon might not speak publicly. Stephen, who apparently was the chief deacon, was described in the Scriptures as a man "full of faith and power" who "did great wonders and signs among the people" (Acts 6:8). He was an excellent orator who was highly skilled in presenting the gospel. He became the first martyr as the result of his speaking boldly about Jesus to the Jewish religious council.

Stephen, however, did not have preaching and prayer as his first job description. He exercised his spiritual gifts in the office of deacon; his primary role was to oversee the meeting of practical needs, not to set the spiritual agenda for the church.

Being a servant does not mean that one relinquishes all of one's spiritual gifts and abilities; rather, it means that one uses those gifts and exercises those abilities within the functional parameters and goals established by one who is in a position of greater authority.

An effective servant is one who *always* submits his will to those who are in authority over him. We each are in a line of authority; no person lives without having someone in authority over him. Ultimately for the Christian, that authority is Christ Jesus. It is only when we learn to submit our wills to His will and to obey those whom God has placed over us that we truly can be effective servants.

A rebellious person might go through some of the external motions of service for a period of time, but unless his rebellious spirit is broken into submission by the Holy Spirit, the person will not *remain* a steadfast servant over time. A rebellious person looks for a way out of service anytime things don't go his way or he cannot be in control of a situation. A rebellious person cannot be truly effective in helping people grow in their faith or experience an increasing reliance upon the Holy Spirit because the rebellious person is not totally reliant upon the Holy Spirit himself. A faithful, obedient person is willing to "let go and let God," whereas a rebellious person has an attitude of "hold control tightly or do it myself."

Submission is not a state of groveling or of weakness, as we tend to think in our modern American culture. Rather, it is recognizing that someone has greater God-given authority in a particular situation. It is a yielding of one's decision-making power to a higher authority, a curbing of one's behavior to conform to the rule established by one who occupies a greater position.

• *How do you feel when you submit yourself to a higher authority?*

free —

Submissiveness and faith are closely linked. If you fail to believe that God is going to provide for you, protect you, or work things for good on your behalf, you are unlikely to submit to God or trust

Him. If you believe that God is your heavenly Father and that all He does is ultimately for your blessing and eternal good, then you are likely to submit to Him and to have faith in Him, trusting Him for every detail of your life.

The first deacons were willing to let the apostles be apostles and to take on their own role of service as deacons. They did not try to lead the church, but they tried to resolve the problems within the church under the authority granted to them by the apostles.

As servants today, we are not called to make our own spiritual decisions but, rather, to submit ourselves to the Holy Spirit and to do only what He directs us to say, do, and decide.

Having a submissive spirit is important regardless of a person's rank or position. A senior pastor or denominational leader must be no less submissive in spirit than the newest convert to Christ. The position one holds does not alter the state that must exist in one's heart. Jesus recognized a Roman centurion as being one of the most submissive and faith-filled people He encountered during His ministry (Matt. 8:5–13).

What the Word Says	What the Word Says to Me
Now when Jesus had entered Capernaum, a centurion came to Him, pleading with Him, saying, "Lord, my servant is lying at home paralyzed, dreadfully tormented."	-----------
And Jesus said to him, "I will come and heal him."	-----------
The centurion answered and said, "Lord, I am not worthy that You should come under my roof. But only speak a word, and my servant will be healed. For I also am a man under authority, having soldiers under me. And I say to this one, 'Go,' and he goes; and to	-----------

another, 'Come,' and he comes;
and to my servant, 'Do this,' and
he does it."

When Jesus heard it, He mar-
veled, and said to those who
followed, "Assuredly, I say to you,
I have not found such great faith,
not even in Israel!" . . . Then Jesus
said to the centurion, "Go your
way; and as you have believed, so
let it be done for you." And his
servant was healed that same hour
(Matt. 8:5–10,13).

I urge you, brethren—you know
the household of Stephanas, that
it is the firstfruits of Achaia, and
that they have devoted themselves
to the ministry of the saints—that
you also submit to such, and to
everyone who works and labors
with us.

I am glad about the coming of
Stephanas, Fortunatus, and
Achaicus, for what was lacking on
your part they supplied. For they
refreshed my spirit and yours.
Therefore acknowledge such men
(1 Cor. 16:15–18).

Submit to God (James 4:7).

Therefore submit yourselves to
every ordinance of man for the
Lord's sake, whether to the king
as supreme, or to governors, as to
those who are sent by him for the
punishment of evildoers and for
the praise of those who do good.

For this is the will of God, that by doing good you may put to silence the ignorance of foolish men—as free, yet not using liberty as a cloak for vice, but as bondservants of God (1 Peter 2:13–16).

• *What new insights from the Bible do you have into what it means to be submissive?*

• *In what ways are you feeling challenged by God's Spirit?*

Being submissive

The Quality of a Good Reputation

The deacons were chosen first and foremost because they were "men of good reputation." They had exemplary character and were men of the highest integrity.

A good reputation is something we each are to work at achieving and to value highly. A "good name" is a tremendous asset.

Having a good reputation does not mean that people will totally agree with you at all times, or you with them. You may disagree with the decisions made by a person of good character and still admire and respect a person as a man or woman of God.

From the biblical point of view, goodness and godliness are the same. One cannot bear a reputation for goodness without being godly; a godly person is good. Goodness is one of the qualities of the Holy Spirit that we are to bear as His fruit in our lives (Gal. 5:22).

People judge a person's reputation on the basis of what that person says and does. The fact is, what you believe is inevitably revealed by what you say, and what you say inevitably dictates what you do. When what a person says he believes and what he does are one and the same, there's a consistency to the person's life that is obvious to all—Christian and sinner alike.

If a person believes God's Word, says that he is making God's Word his way of life, and then truly attempts to live out God's Word on a daily basis, that person is building a good reputation.

A good reputation has nothing to do with the standards of success established by the world. Being rich, famous, or the leader of an organization does not necessarily make a person good or godly. The lowliest wage earner can be a person of excellent reputation. The most unrecognized person within the church might still be a person about whom all say, "That is a godly person."

Why is a good reputation so vital for service? Because genuine service is a reflection of God's love and presence. If a person is going through the motions of service but is doing so with an evil intent, a mixed motive, or a selfish interest, the person receiving the service will know it. Not only will the provider of the service be suspect, but the service itself will be suspect.

In our culture today, many have the opinion, "It doesn't matter about the character of the person as long as the outcome of his or her work is good." From God's standpoint, the character of the person giving the service *is* what makes the outcome of that person's work good! You cannot separate inner character and outer deeds. You can gloss over the difference, but in the end, a good reputation is vital to good service.

A person's reputation is one of the foremost factors in that person's witness to the world about the saving grace of God and the empowerment and presence of the Holy Spirit. A person's greatest witness for Christ is found in the way a person lives his or her daily life. Who you are, from the inside out, is the platform on which you give service. Your service will not redeem you or make your reputation. Your reputation for having a godly character is what will redeem your service and give you a witness for Christ Jesus.

We must also be aware that a good reputation does not necessarily spare a person from persecution (2 Tim. 3:12–15). Those who perform good service to others sometimes are criticized for it, misunderstood because of it, or ridiculed as being a "goody two-shoes." What can be said for a good reputation, however, is that it survives persecution—even if that persecution leads to death. A good reputation lasts, and it impacts others for good. If a person's reputation is a godly one in Christ Jesus, it will last into eternity.

If you desire for your service to outlive your lifetime and to be credited to your eternal reward, you must be a person who strives to achieve and maintain a good reputation. Don't be discouraged if you face persecution or if your reputation is assaulted for the service you perform. Press on. Your reputation *will* be vindicated eventually, and your service *will* be rewarded by God.

> • *How do you feel if a "bad person" does a good thing for you? What is likely to be your response to the person, and to the service he or she rendered to you?*

_____

_____

What the Word Says	What the Word Says to Me
The fruit of the Spirit is . . . goodness (Gal. 5:22).	---------------------------- ----------------------------
A good name is to be chosen rather than great riches (Prov. 22:1).	---------------------------- ----------------------------
Every good tree bears good fruit, but a bad tree bears bad fruit. A good tree cannot bear bad fruit, nor can a bad tree bear good fruit (Matt. 7:17–18).	---------------------------- ---------------------------- ---------------------------- ---------------------------- ----------------------------
All who desire to live godly in Christ Jesus will suffer persecution. But evil men and impostors will grow worse and worse, deceiving and being deceived. But you must continue in the things which you have learned and been assured of, knowing from whom	---------------------------- ---------------------------- ---------------------------- ---------------------------- ---------------------------- ---------------------------- ----------------------------

you have learned them, and that
from childhood you have known
the Holy Scriptures, which are
able to make you wise for salvation through faith which is in
Christ Jesus (2 Tim. 3:12–15).

We should live soberly, righ-
teously, and godly in the present
age (Titus 2:12).

I have no greater joy than to hear
that my children walk in truth.
Beloved, you do faithfully whatever you do for the brethren and
for strangers, who have borne witness of your love before the
church. If you send them forward
on their journey in a manner worthy of God, you will do well
(3 John 4–6).

• *What new insights do you have into the importance of having a
godly reputation?*

_____

_____

• *In what ways are you being spiritually challenged?*

_____

_____

The Quality of Being Full of the Holy Spirit

The apostles requested that the members of the Jerusalem church
choose as deacons men who were "full of the Holy Spirit" (Acts
6:3).

As believers, the Holy Spirit is the One who guides us into all good words, good works, and a good walk before our heavenly Father. He is the One who enables or empowers us to perform good works that have a lasting benefit to the kingdom of God. It is virtually impossible to do anything on this earth that is of eternal value unless one is enabled by the Holy Spirit to do that work.

God alone knows which of your works has the potential to be the most effective and productive in His kingdom. He alone guarantees that your work succeeds, in spite of persecution and your own lack of ability or failures. God alone can cause a work of service to become a point of witness to a lost soul and can use your service to redeem lives for all eternity. God alone can assure you of an eternal reward for your service. Without God, nothing that you do can be remotely as important, beneficial, or lasting as what you do *with* God.

We already mentioned the deacon Stephen described in Acts 6 as being a man who was, "full of faith and the Holy Spirit" and "full of faith and power" (Acts 6:5, 8). What an amazing and wonderful reputation to have! To be *full* of God's Spirit means that Stephen's life was overflowing and continuously manifesting the very qualities of the character of God. He was a man who embodied all of the fruit of the Spirit described by Paul: love, joy, peace, longsuffering, kindness, goodness, faithfulness, gentleness, and self-control (Gal. 5:22–23). Paul also wrote that there's nothing in the law—either God's law or man's law—that prohibits a person from manifesting these traits. They are qualities of character that are desirable in *all* people, in *all* periods of history, and in young and old believers alike.

A servant who is full of the Holy Spirit is a man or woman who is like Jesus, Himself full of the Holy Spirit from the moment of His birth. A person filled with the Holy Spirit is one who says what Jesus would say in any given situation, do what Jesus would do to impact any given circumstance, and live as Jesus would live in any environment.

A servant who is full of the Holy Spirit is obviously one who is completely submissive to the Holy Spirit for direction, guidance, and power. He does nothing that the Holy Spirit does not prompt and enable. He is totally reliant upon God for every breath he takes and every move he makes.

Christians often say to one another, "If only Jesus were here, He'd remedy this situation." The fact is, if we are truly full of the same Holy Spirit that filled Jesus, then it's as if Jesus is in our midst. And our collective service or ministry to others will be just as effective and meaningful as if that person were touched by the very hands of Christ Jesus, heard the very words of Christ Jesus, or received the very gifts that Christ Jesus would give.

When we attempt to serve others without relying upon the Holy Spirit, we burn out, become discouraged at failures and persecutions, and often become lax in our service and weak in our desire to serve. None of us can remain faithful, devoted, consistent, and persistent in our service without the Holy Spirit's help.

To be truly effective in your service to others, you must ask the Holy Spirit to work in you and through you—today, tomorrow, and every day in your future.

> • *Have you had an experience in which you attempted to do a "good work" without first consulting or relying upon the Holy Spirit? What were the long-range results—in you, as well as in those you served?*

> • *Have you had an experience in which you know you were 100 percent reliant upon and empowered by the Holy Spirit in your service? What were the long-range results—in you, and in those you served?*

What the Word Says

The fruit of the Spirit is love, joy, peace, longsuffering, kindness, goodness, faithfulness, gentleness, self-control. Against such there is no law (Gal. 5:22–23).

What the Word Says to Me

• *In what ways are you being challenged in your spirit?*

_____

_____

•*What new insights do you have into the qualities of character that are associated with effective service?*

_____

_____

LESSON 7

THE QUALITIES OF AN EFFECTIVE SERVANT: PART 2

When the first church body in Jerusalem faced very practical material needs, the apostles were led by the Holy Spirit to tell the multitude of believers to choose seven men to function as deacons. In the last lesson, we covered three of the traits that these deacons were to embody in their service: submissiveness, a good reputation, and a life filled with the Holy Spirit. In this lesson, we will cover the remaining traits that were considered vital for a person to truly be an effective "servant" to God's people.

These character-trait qualities are identified as the qualities of effective service within the church, but they are also the qualities that are most effective in serving others in order to bring them to Christ. A godly person who simultaneously has a submissive human spirit and is filled with the power of the Holy Spirit is an extremely effective witness for Christ. Such a person is a "model believer," a man or woman who has a tremendous role in the growth and development of God's kingdom, regardless of the specific function or role that person may have. Show me a godly janitor who is submissive to those in authority over him but is also filled with God's Holy Spirit, and I will show you a person who truly makes a lasting difference for good, both in the church and in the world at large. Show me a senior pastor who has an "I-can-do-it-on-my-own" attitude and who is not reliant upon the Holy Spirit, and I will show you a person who is likely in error in various areas of his personal life. His reputation, his attitude, and his lack of the fruit of the Holy Spirit in his life will eventually harm the church and be of virtually no benefit to the world in the long run.

No matter what job you hold, in the church or in the world, you are called to be a servant who embodies the character traits that were required of the first deacons. If you are to serve others and do so effectively, as they were commissioned to do, then you must bear the same spiritual integrity that they manifested.

The Quality of Wisdom

The first deacons chosen by the church were to be men who were full of wisdom (Acts 6:3).

Wisdom is knowing both what God desires for a person to do and how God desires for the job to be done, and then having the courage actually to *do* what is required. Stated another way: What a person does and the degree to which his or her actions are successful in meeting God's goals are a measure of that person's wisdom.

You cannot be wise and say nothing or do nothing. How will anybody know you are wise? How will *you* know you are wise? Wisdom is not simply having head knowledge. It is having *application* knowledge—knowing how, when, where, and to whom to apply one's knowledge of God's purposes, plans, and commandments. Wisdom is knowledge that is lived out, acted upon, and made useful to real-life problems, decisions, needs, and challenges.

Wisdom comes from God. It flows from the Holy Spirit to us as we rely upon the Holy Spirit for it. God doesn't pour out His wisdom on people who don't want it or request it. At the same time, He is more than willing to pour out His wisdom in generous portions, and without any recrimination, on those who do desire it and ask for it. If you want more wisdom, ask God to give it to you!

Wisdom is vital for service and especially for service in the church, because without it *God's* answer to human problems is not manifested. Service can be rendered solely from fleshly desires and from human levels of intelligence and ability, but such service is limited and often ineffectual or even in error. Can you imagine what might have happened if the early church had simply chosen the smartest men they knew, but not necessarily the wisest men they knew? They likely would have had a catastrophe because they would have had seven highly "intelligent" opinions about how to serve and what to do, but no consensus in the Spirit and no true unity in purpose, plan, or result. They would have had rule by committee, rather than order established by a consensus of faith about what the Holy Spirit was directing them to do.

• *Have you ever been the victim of someone's "bright idea"—an idea that later was revealed to be out of alignment with what the Holy Spirit desired?*

Wisdom is something we need on a daily basis. It is often related very directly to a particular question, problem, or need. Ask the Holy Spirit every morning to give you the wisdom you will need to deal with the circumstances and situations that you will face in the coming day. As you face particular decisions, ask the Holy Spirit to guide you. As you encounter people throughout your day, ask the Holy Spirit to direct your conversation. You can never ask too much or too often for God's wisdom.

We must ask for wisdom in faith (James 1:6). After you have prayed for wisdom, make the decision or take the action that you believe God has called you to do. Don't second-guess God or yourself at that point. God will reveal to you if you have erred. The only way to grow in your ability to apply God's Word effectively is to obey what God speaks to your heart. Keep in mind always that the Holy Spirit will never direct you to do something that is contrary to God's Word, the Bible.

What the Word Says	What the Word Says to Me
If any of you lacks wisdom, let him ask of God, who gives to all liberally and without reproach, and it will be given to him. But let him ask in faith, with no doubting (James 1:5–6).	------------------------------ ------------------------------ ------------------------------ ------------------------------ ------------------------------ ------------------------------
The wisdom that is from above is first pure, then peaceable, gentle, willing to yield, full of mercy and good fruits, without partiality and without hypocrisy (James 3:17).	------------------------------ ------------------------------ ------------------------------ ------------------------------ ------------------------------ ------------------------------
The fear of the LORD is the beginning of wisdom, And the knowledge of the Holy One is understanding (Prov. 9:10).	------------------------------ ------------------------------ ------------------------------ ------------------------------
And my speech and my preaching were not with persuasive words of human wisdom, but in demonstration of the Spirit and of power, that your faith should not be in the wisdom of men but in the power of God (1 Cor. 2:4–5).	------------------------------ ------------------------------ ------------------------------ ------------------------------ ------------------------------ ------------------------------ ------------------------------

•*What new insights do you have into the importance of wisdom to godly service?*

_____

_____

• *In what ways are you feeling challenged in your spirit?*

_____

_____

The Quality of Vision

The deacons chosen by the early church were men who had a vision for what God desired to be done in their midst. They were not attempting to fulfill their own desires or goals but, rather, the desires of God's heart for His people.

True service always has an evangelistic, outward reach to it that is borne of a vision for what God desires to do on the earth. We each are responsible for winning as many people as possible to Christ Jesus in our generation. When we have this at the core of our desire to serve, everything that we do takes on greater meaning.

A person with a vision for the greater plans and purposes of God is a person who finds meaning and fulfillment in even the most mundane of tasks. For example, we are not to feed people simply to feed people. We are to feed the hungry so that with full stomachs, they might fully receive the gospel of Christ. We are not to provide clothing, shelter, or medical help to people merely so they can be warm, comfortable, protected from the elements, and live longer. We are to engage in these forms of service so that people might not have any practical, material, or physical impediments that keep them from clearly hearing God's call of love, grace, and forgiveness to them. True Christian service involves removing the obstacles that keep a person from having "ears to hear" and "eyes to see."

Without very practical, daily service being performed by the deacons in the early church, it is very likely that large numbers of needy Christians would have fallen away from their newfound faith. The Christian life would simply have been too difficult for them—their needs would have loomed so large that they would not have been able to hear with open hearts the full message of the gospel that was being presented to them by the apostles.

A vision grows in us when we ask ourselves *why* God has called us to help others. We see the bigger picture: God desires to meet the needs of all people and to show His love to us in practical, tangible ways. God blesses His people materially, practically, and physically as much as He blesses His people spiritually. So often we place such great importance upon God's spiritual blessing—which, indeed, is the greater blessing because it is eternal—that we neglect to give importance to God's material blessings extended to those who are lacking adequate provision and protection, the basics necessary for life. Jesus said that He came not only to give us eternal life but an abundant life in the here and now (John 10:10). As His servants, we are to provide service that leads both to an abundant life on this earth and to a spiritual life that is everlasting.

One form of service is not to be replaced by the other. Rather, we are to have a vision for the greater service—leading a person to Christ—as we engage diligently in performing the practical service of meeting daily needs.

> • *Have you ever encountered a person who seemed so "heavenly minded" that he or she was of little earthly good—doing virtually nothing practical to further God's Kingdom? How did you feel?*

_____

_____

> •*What new insights do you have into the importance of having a vision from God for the service you render to others?*

_____

_____

What the Word Says

I have become all things to all men, that I might by all means save some. Now this I do for the gospel's sake, that I may be partaker of it with you (1 Cor. 9:22–23).

If I do not do the works of My Father, do not believe Me; but if I do, though you do not believe Me, believe the works, that you may know and believe that the Father s in Me, and I in Him (John 10:37–38).

What the Word Says to Me

_____

_____

_____

_____

_____

_____

_____

_____

_____

_____

_____

_____

_____

The glory which You gave Me I
have given them, that they may be
one just as We are one: I in them,
and You in Me; that they may be
made perfect in one, and that the
world may know that You have
sent Me, and have loved them as
You have loved Me (John
17:22–23).

The Quality of Humility

Perhaps the supreme character trait of all those manifested by the deacons in the first-century church was humility. These men who were filled with faith and power, who had a vision for God's work to be done, and who had outstanding reputations were asked to *serve tables*. They were asked to become, in effect, waiters. They were responsible for making certain that everyone at the communal meals held by the church received enough food and that their needs were met without prejudice or favoritism.

Many of the most important roles in the church today—the roles that keep a church functioning at peak performance week after week—are roles similar to that of serving tables. Show me ushers, greeters, parking attendants, hospitality hostesses, and janitors who do their work with the same spirit as that of the first deacons, and I will show you a church that is headed for great effectiveness in the winning of souls and the building up of the body of Christ.

Humility is at the foundation of submissiveness. It is the complement character trait to wisdom—it is what keeps the wise from becoming arrogant. Humility is a sign of being filled with the Holy Spirit; it is a hallmark among those who have good reputations. Humility says, "Not my will, but Your will"; it is the trait that opens one's eyes to the broader vision that God has for a human life.

Humility will cause a person to see every task as a "job" to be done for God, rather than as a "position" to be filled to win the approval of men.

In serving tables, the deacons had this as their goal: "See that everybody is taken care of"—not just in this hour, but throughout this week, and on through this month, this year, and forever. "Seeing that everybody is taken care of" is one of the best definitions of service I have ever heard. When we serve an individual, we are actually serving the greater body of Christ. Any form of service that we desire to render to the church as a whole we must first render to an individual.

It is not enough that a person be fed once. A person must be fed consistently so that hunger is no longer a part of that person's daily concern. It is not enough that a person be greeted warmly on one Sunday a year. A person must feel welcome within the church body every time he sets foot inside the church or encounters a member of the church. It is not enough that a person be "told" the gospel once. A person must be presented with the gospel at all times—in every word, by every deed, and through every action that is taken on behalf of that person.

Humility calls us to see the *person* who needs our help, not the crowd who might shower adoration upon us.

Pride and service are incompatible. Pride is self-seeking. Service seeks out the best for others.

Pride insists on having its own way. Service makes a way for others.

Pride demands recognition. Service works for results.

Pride fills us up with self-importance. Service empties us of self.

If we are willing to bow our knees before God, we must also be willing to get down on our knees to help others. Humility before God must extend to our having a humble spirit before men.

> • *Have you ever been helped by a person with a proud spirit? By a person with a humble spirit? How did each person make you feel? What was your response to him or her?*

_____

_____

> •*What new insights do you have into the relationship between service and humility?*

_____

_____

What the Word Says	**What the Word Says to Me**
Be submissive to one another, and be clothed with humility, for "God resists the proud, But gives grace to the humble." Therefore humble yourselves under the mighty hand of God, that He may exalt you in due time (1 Peter 5:5–6).	------------------------------
We urge you, brethren, to recognize those who labor among you, and are over you in the Lord and admonish you, and to esteem them very highly in love for their work's sake. Be at peace among yourselves (1 Thess. 5:12–13).	------------------------------
And what does the LORD require of you But to do justly, To love mercy, And to walk humbly with your God? (Micah 6:8).	------------------------------
Humble yourselves in the sight of the Lord, and He will lift you up (James 4:10).	------------------------------
Let nothing be done through selfish ambition or conceit, but in lowliness of mind let each esteem others better than himself. Let each of you look out not only for his own interests, but also for the interests of others (Phil. 2:3–4).	------------------------------

• *In what ways are you feeling challenged in your spirit?*

_____

_____

The Result of Genuine Service

What was the result of the church's choosing deacons who bore these six qualities: submissiveness, good reputation, full of the Holy Spirit, wisdom, a vision for the work of God, and humility? Acts 6:7 tells us:

> The word of God spread, and the number of the disciples multiplied greatly in Jerusalem, and a great many of the priests were obedient to the faith.

A church that is filled with people who are active in their service one to another is a church that is like a great magnet to lost souls. The reputation of that church spreads quickly. Christ is lifted up on the shoulders of men and women who are kneeling to perform good service to others. He draws the lost to Himself through the extended arms of believers.

Note that the Bible says a great many of the *priests* became obedient to the faith. The service of the deacons became an example to the believers. They, in turn, began to serve one another with generous, humble, submissive spirits that were open to the Holy Spirit's wisdom and power. As the believers began to serve, the world took notice. The entire atmosphere of Jerusalem changed. Those who were engaged in the priestly functions of the temple actually gained heart at what they felt, saw, and heard. They began to *mean* what they had been doing—they began to love God with all of their hearts, minds, and souls. Many of them began to claim Jesus as Messiah.

If you want to bring joy to the heart of your pastor today, begin to serve others in your church as if you are serving Jesus Himself. Pour out your love to your fellow believers. Not only will your example draw unbelievers to your church fellowship, but your pastor will be encouraged as never before. You'll see a change in the way he preaches, teaches, and leads your congregation. Nothing warms the heart of a pastor more than to see those in his congregation loving one another as the deacons surely loved the believers in that first-century church.

If you want to see church growth, begin with service. It flows automatically from hearts that bear the qualities of submissiveness, godly character, wisdom, a vision for God's work, humility, and a desire to be filled to overflowing with God's Spirit.

> • *In what ways are you feeling challenged to serve others as the first deacons served the church?*

_____

_____

LESSON 8

EQUIPPED FOR SERVICE

People offer any number of excuses for not engaging in active service to others. Some say that they don't have time; others say that they have other priorities. The two basic reasons, however, that I see at the *root* of why people don't serve are these:

1. *Pride*. They simply don't want to humble themselves to serve others. Selfishness is a form of pride—people don't want to be inconvenienced or detoured from what they want to do, when they want to do it. Self-centeredness is pride.

2. *Fear of failure*. Many people feel that they don't have anything to give to others or that others will not be open to receiving what they can offer or desire to offer.

Ultimately, the person who steadfastly refuses to engage in service is a person who

• . . . *doesn't understand who God is.* If a person truly has an understanding of God as a loving, generous Father—One who gave His only begotten Son so that we might be reconciled to Him and live with Him forever—then a person has a built-in desire to give. How can a person know the extent of God's love and not want to share it with others? God not only requires us to give service, He desires for us to give service. If we know from our own experience of salvation that God is love, then we must also know that as God's Spirit resides within us, we must love others. That means serving others and giving to others in order to meet their needs.

• . . . *doesn't understand why he or she is alive.* So many people today question, "Why am I here?" The Christian should never have to ask that question. If you are a follower of Jesus Christ, you are alive on this earth to worship God and to reflect glory to God by the way you serve your fellow man. Loving God and loving others, just as you love your own life, is the commandment of God to you. It is your purpose, your job, your role, your position, your meaning in life.

• . . . *doesn't understand God's purpose for this world.* God's purpose for the world is that all men might come to know God and receive forgiveness through Christ Jesus. Jesus came to seek and to save *all* who are lost. God's purpose for you as a part of the larger body of Christ is that you be a part of an ongoing, consistent, and diligent effort to win lost souls to Christ and to build up the faith of your fellow Christians. God's purpose is that His kingdom be established on earth, just as it is in heaven. Jesus taught us to pray, "Our Father in heaven, / Hallowed be Your name. / Your kingdom come. / Your will be done / On earth as it is in heaven" (Matt. 6:9–10).

If a person truly understands who God is, why he is on this earth, and what God's purposes are for all mankind, how can he dare to say to God, "I'd rather do my own thing than serve You by serving others"? How does he dare to exert his own will over God's will?

I have much more compassion for those who don't believe they have any talents to give to God than I have for those who know they are talented and who refuse to use their talents for God's glory.

My word to those of you who believe that you don't have anything to offer in the way of service is this: *You do.* God does not call any person to do anything within His kingdom unless He also equips that person—spiritually, materially, physically, mentally, financially, and in all other ways. For whatever type of service God may be opening up to you, God not only has prepared you and equipped you to succeed in doing it, but He will continue to assist you and increase your talents as you engage in the work set before you.

> • *In what ways are you feeling challenged by the Holy Spirit right now?*

_____

_____

Created for Service

Service is a part of God's reason for creating you. Ephesians 2:10 tells us,

> We are His workmanship, created in Christ Jesus for good works, which God prepared beforehand that we should walk in them.

Even before you were born, God had in mind who you would be and what He would desire for you to do in this very specific time and situation in which you are living right now. You haven't arrived where you are in your life by accident or whim. God's plan and purpose for you are unfolding. God would not intend for you to engage in service for Him without preparing you for the challenge.

Your service is an outgrowth of the talents and abilities that God has placed in your life. We each have been given certain "service-ready equipment" from birth: a unique personality, mental and emotional capacities and propensities, talents, and strengths.

God has been at work in your life from your first moments, molding and preparing you to fulfill His plan and purpose for you. Throughout our lives, God has allowed us to have certain experiences, engage in certain relationships, and be a part of certain groups of people in certain environments and cultures—all of which become a part of the mix of who we are and what we bring to any form of ministry or service. We can be assured that He will continue to work in us until the day we die.

God works in us and through us as we serve, and He uses our service to continue to prepare us for even greater service in the days ahead.

You may feel that you are at the kindergarten level of service—that you have limited resources and abilities with which to serve. God's plan is that you use what you have been given to the fullest, and in the course of your using those resources and abilities, He will *increase* them so that you are able to serve Him with greater and greater abilities, and do so more and more effectively.

God's purpose for you in service is never to decrease you or to diminish you but, rather, to increase you and to cause you to prosper in all areas of your life mentally, physically, emotionally, materially, relationally, and above all, spiritually.

> • *Reflect back over your life and isolate several examples of how God has equipped you for service through the talents, experiences, skills, and capacities He has given you and helped you to develop.*

_____

_____

What the Word Says	What the Word Says to Me
Now may the God of peace who brought up our Lord Jesus from the dead, that great Shepherd of the sheep, through the blood of the everlasting covenant, make you complete in every good work to do His will, working in you what is well pleasing in His sight, through Jesus Christ, to whom be glory forever and ever. Amen (Heb. 13:20–21).	_____ _____ _____ _____ _____ _____ _____ _____ _____ _____
Therefore we also, since we are surrounded by so great a cloud of witnesses, let us lay aside every weight, and the sin which so easily	_____ _____ _____ _____

ensnares us, and let us run with
endurance the race that is set
before us, looking unto Jesus the
author and finisher of our faith
(Heb. 12:1–2).

He who has begun a good work in
you will complete it until the day
of Jesus Christ (Phil. 1:6).

• *How do you feel in knowing that God is at work in you and through*
you as you serve others?

• *In what ways are you feeling challenged in your spirit?*

Equipped with Spiritual Gifts

Not only have you been equipped with certain natural gifts and
abilities, but the Holy Spirit dwells within you. He brings to you
His unlimited gifts and abilities! That's why Paul could claim so
boldly, "I can do all things through Christ who strengthens me"
(Phil. 4:13).

What you lack, the Holy Spirit supplies.

When you are weak, He is strong.

When you err or fail in your service to others, He has the capacity to continue to work all things together for good—both to you
and to those whom you serve (Rom. 8:28).

Indeed, if God is for us, who can be against us (Rom. 8:31)? We are
guaranteed to be successful in our service to others as long as we
rely upon the Holy Spirit to work in us, through us, and on our behalf—
not only individually but as members of the greater body of Christ.

Paul cites several types of spiritual gifts that the Holy Spirit gives
freely to those who believe in Christ Jesus and are filled with the Spirit.

In Romans 12:6–8 Paul lists several gifts:

> Having then gifts differing according to the grace that is given to us, let us use them: if prophecy, let us prophesy in proportion to our faith; or ministry, let us use it in our ministering; he who teaches, in teaching; he who exhorts, in exhortation; he who gives, with liberality; he who leads, with diligence; he who shows mercy, with cheerfulness.

Note that Paul's emphasis is on the *use* of spiritual gifts. What the Holy Spirit gives to us we are to *use* for the benefit of others. They are not gifts given to us for our exclusive benefit or enjoyment but, rather, that others might benefit and, in the process, we might grow in our faith and spiritual power.

Furthermore, it is the Holy Spirit who determines which gift of *His* He will choose to put into operation at any given time in our lives and service to others. The gifts of the Spirit are just that—the Spirit's gifts. They reside in Him and are given to us for the greater use of the entire body of Christ. We see this clearly as Paul describes some of the gifts in 1 Corinthians 12:4–11:

> There are diversities of gifts, but the same Spirit. There are differences of ministries, but the same Lord. And there are diversities of activities, but it is the same God who works all in all. But the manifestation of the Spirit is given to each one for the profit of all: for to one is given the word of wisdom through the Spirit, to another the word of knowledge through the same Spirit, to another faith by the same Spirit, to another gifts of healings by the same Spirit, to another the working of miracles, to another prophecy, to another discerning of spirits, to another different kinds of tongues, to another the interpretation of tongues. But one and the same Spirit works all these things, distributing to each one individually as He wills.

God gifts us with supernatural gifts so that we might serve others. If you feel a need arising in your service to another person, ask God to endow you with whatever gift you need in order to get

His job done for *His* glory. He will do so! He is the One who gives spiritual gifts so that His people might be edified and His kingdom expanded and His love and grace revealed to the lost.

> •*What new insights do you have into God's spiritual gifts and their relationship to your service of others?*

_____

_____

What the Word Says	What the Word Says to Me
Now may He who supplies seed to the sower, and bread for food, supply and multiply the seed you have sown and increase the fruits of your righteousness, while you are enriched in everything for all liberality, which causes thanksgiving through us to God (2 Cor. 9:10–11).	_____ _____ _____ _____ _____ _____ _____ _____
Pursue love, and desire spiritual gifts, but especially that you may prophesy. . . . He who prophesies speaks edification and exhortation and comfort to men (1 Cor. 14:1, 3).	_____ _____ _____ _____ _____
For it is God who works in you both to will and to do for His good pleasure (Phil. 2:13).	_____ _____ _____

The Purpose of Gifts

Paul wrote this to the Corinthians:

> Blessed be the God and Father of our Lord Jesus Christ, the Father of mercies and God of all comfort, who comforts

us in all our tribulation, that we may be able to comfort those
who are in any trouble, with the comfort with which we ourselves are comforted by God. (2 Cor. 1:3–4)

The gifts of the Holy Spirit—both those given to us as natural
endowments from our birth and throughout our lives, as well as
those that the Holy Spirit gives to us for the meeting of specific
needs and situations—are intended for us to use in comforting
those who are in trouble. As we have been comforted by Christ, so
we are to comfort others.

All of our experiences in life—and especially those which have
brought us pain, sorrow, and suffering—equip us in unique ways
to have empathy with others and to show compassion to them.
Everything in your life, and perhaps especially your failures and
trials, has in some way prepared you to show the love of God to
others in ways that are more heartfelt, meaningful, and effective.
God's grace to you in your past times of suffering prepares you
to become an effective minister of God to those who are currently
suffering.

Too often, the laymen in a church expect the pastor to do all of
the ministering to those who have emotional or spiritual needs.
That is far from what the Bible sets as the standard for service.
Read what Paul wrote to the Ephesians:

To each one of us grace was given according to the measure
of Christ's gift. . . . And He Himself gave some to be apostles, some prophets, some evangelists, and some pastors and
teachers, for the equipping of the saints for the work of ministry, for the edifying of the body of Christ, till we all come
to the unity of the faith and of the knowledge of the Son
of God, to a perfect man, to the measure of the stature of
the fullness of Christ. (Eph. 4:7, 11–13)

The leaders in any church setting—those called to be apostles,
prophets, evangelists, pastors, and teachers—are placed there for
one main reason: *to equip the saints for the work of ministry*. If you
are a layman, you are a saint who is being equipped for ministry.

Your purpose in life is not to listen to hundreds of sermons and attend dozens of seminars and then die and go to heaven. Your purpose is to hear the Word of God as it is preached and taught to you and then immediately and consistently to apply that preaching and teaching in practical forms of service to the people around you. The "work" of ministry belongs to all of God's people. In ministering to others, you become an agent of God's comfort and care.

• *What new insights do you have into your role of service and into who is called to be a "minister"?*

———————————————————————————————

———————————————————————————————

None of us can justify our existence apart from God. We each are deeply indebted to God for every blessing He has given us— every bit of help He has given in times of trouble, every bit of consolation and comfort He has given in times of pain and sorrow, and every bit of encouragement He has given in times of failure.

It is out of a heart of thanksgiving for what God has done for us that we, in turn, serve others. If you have thanksgiving in your heart . . . if you have been forgiven by God and are the recipient of God's love . . . then you *are* equipped for service. What you lack in ability, He will provide.

• *In what ways are you feeling challenged in your faith walk today?*

———————————————————————————————

———————————————————————————————

LESSON 9

FIVE PRINCIPLES FROM GOD'S WORD ABOUT SUCCESSFUL SERVICE

Service is a theme that runs throughout God's Word from cover to cover. The Bible is filled with countless examples of ways in which God served His people, ways in which God's people served God and others, and commandments that are related to service. In this lesson, we are going to take a look at five principles from God's Word that are related to service. These principles are interrelated and should be taken as a whole.

As you study these principles you will be challenged repeatedly to ask tough questions of yourself. Why am I so insistent in this? Because God has made it very clear in His Word that He *requires* service from us. Service is not an option or a suggestion. It is a commandment.

Service is also our way to increased blessing and fulfillment in life. God does not command us to serve so that we might be hurt, diminished, decreased, or made to suffer. Rather, God commands us to service so that through our service to others, He might reward us, bring us blessing, teach us, and develop a closer relationship with us. God always rewards our service with more of His presence and power and, ultimately, with eternal rewards that are beyond our ability to imagine.

Jesus said, "A servant is not greater than his master; nor is he who is sent greater than he who sent him. If you know these things, blessed are you if you do them" (John 13:16–17). We *must* serve. But this is a command we should delight in doing because service always reaps benefit—to us personally as well as to those whom we serve.

> • *How do you feel about service being a command from God? How do you feel about service being rewarded by God?*

_____

_____

Principle #1: Volunteerism

A true servant doesn't wait to be asked. He or she discerns a need and acts decisively to meet it. A servant has a sensitive heart and a willing spirit.

A volunteer is motivated by love and prompted to action by the presence of a need. A volunteer is *not* motivated by convenience or leisure time. Those who say "someday I'll get involved" or "someday I'll serve God" are offering lame excuses. If you are waiting for a convenient time to serve, you will never serve.

Ask yourself, "What is it that I won't do for God? What is it that I wouldn't do for another person?" An honest answer to those two questions will reveal your own self-pride. Jesus died naked, bloody, and battered, on a cross that was next to a public highway. He was made a laughingstock—a crown of thorns pressed into His brow and a sign above His head labeling Him in mockery, "King of the Jews." Jesus died for *your* sake so that you might have a Savior.

Furthermore, Jesus went to the cross voluntarily. The Bible gives us these words of Jesus, spoken well in advance of His crucifixion:

> I am the good shepherd; and I know My sheep, and am known by My own. As the Father knows Me, even so I know the Father; and I lay down My life for the sheep. . . . I lay down My life that I may take it again. No one takes it from Me, but I lay it down of Myself. I have power to lay it down, and I have power to take it again. This command I have received from My Father. (John 10:14–15, 17–18)

Jesus was obedient to His heavenly Father, and the Cross was His supreme act of volunteerism. He *gave* His life voluntarily for our salvation without regard to pain, suffering, mockery, or the disbelief of many who witnessed His death.

Is there any type of service that is beneath you? Is there anything you won't do for Him?

God said about King David: "I have found David the son of Jesse, a man after My own heart, who will do all My will" (Acts 13:22). Will God say that about you?

What the Word Says

Without your consent I wanted to do nothing, that your good deed might not be by compulsion, as it were, but voluntary (Philem. 14).

Whoever is of a willing heart, let him bring it as an offering to the LORD. . . . They came, both men and women, as many as had a willing heart (Ex. 35:5, 22).

What the Word Says to Me

_____
_____
_____
_____

_____
_____
_____
_____

• *Have you ever been forced to serve others against your will? Have you ever voluntarily served others? How did you feel in each case? What were the outcomes—in your life and in the lives of others?*

_____

_____

Principle #2: Without Comparison

A true servant doesn't compare his level or type of service with that of anyone else. Service is not hierarchical. There is no "top floor, corner office" when it comes to successful service. God looks upon the heart and its motivation, not upon results or achievements, in rewarding service.

As we presented in the last lesson, every person is capable and every person is qualified for some type of service.

Many people say about service, "I'd do more for God if I only had . . ." These are only a few of the excuses given in the "if I only had . . ." category:

- his job and income.
- his circumstances and time availability.
- his opportunities.
- his family background and status.

Everything you have is a gift from God, and God considers what you have been given adequate for the tasks to which He calls you. Rather than focus on what you lack, take a look at what you *have*.

Not only do you have adequate talents and gifts with which to serve, but God has given you a place and a people to serve. God has given you your family, your business or place of employment, your friends, your church, and your neighborhood as opportunities to serve. There are needs all around you. Target *one* of them and get started.

Once you begin to serve, don't criticize those who fail to serve. Jesus did not wash the feet of His disciples and then say to them, "Now you wash My feet." Service must be without criticism and without comparison.

Don't criticize your fellow servants or those who lead your service effort. Encourage them and build them up. The person who gives encouragement is likely the person who receives encouragement. Offer suggestions when you think they may be beneficial to the group as a whole, but don't criticize what a person has done in the past or what he is attempting to do. You never know the full story. Only God knows the full extent of that person's effort and the motivation that is behind it.

What the Word Says	What the Word Says to Me
For we dare not class ourselves or compare ourselves with those who commend themselves. But they, measuring themselves by themselves, and comparing themselves among themselves, are not wise. . . . But "he who glories, let him glory in the LORD." For not he who commends himself is approved, but whom the Lord commends (2 Cor. 10:12, 17–18; also Jer. 9:24).	----------------------------- ----------------------------- ----------------------------- ----------------------------- ----------------------------- ----------------------------- ----------------------------- ----------------------------- -----------------------------
Comfort each other and edify one another. . . . always pursue what is good both for yourselves and for all (1 Thess. 5:11, 15).	----------------------------- ----------------------------- ----------------------------- ----------------------------- -----------------------------

• *Have you ever compared your efforts with those of others and felt unworthy as the result? Have you compared your efforts at service and found others to be lacking? What were the outcomes of your comparisons?*

Principle #3: No Exclusions

If a person volunteers to join you in your service to others, allow him or her the privilege of doing so. Nobody is ever too young to serve or too old. In fact, there's no retirement program for Christian service. Following the Lord's example, we each are to serve the Lord and to serve others every day of our lives.

Jesus called His disciples "little children" during the Last Supper and said to them, "A new commandment I give to you, that you love one another; as I have loved you, that you also love one another. By this all will know that you are My disciples, if you have love for one another" (John 13:34–35). Love knows no age limitations. Even a young child is capable of expressing love and care to others.

Just as you exclude no person from an opportunity to serve, you must not exclude anyone from receiving service. Consider all whom the Lord Jesus touched with His hands. They included a leper, a child, and a blind man. He used His hands to wash the feet of His disciples. Eventually, He spread His hands out on a cross and died for the sins of all mankind. He certainly expects you to extend your hands to those in need regardless of their race, color, culture, or type of need.

What the Word Says	What the Word Says to Me
For there is one God and one Mediator between God and men, the Man Christ Jesus, who gave Himself a ransom for all (1 Tim. 2:5–6).	------------------------------ ------------------------------ ------------------------------ ------------------------------ ------------------------------
For the love of Christ compels us, because we judge thus: that if One died for all, then all died; and He died for all, that those who live should live no longer for themselves, but for Him who died for them and rose again.	------------------------------ ------------------------------ ------------------------------ ------------------------------ ------------------------------ ------------------------------ ------------------------------
Therefore, from now on, we regard no one according to the flesh. . . . God was in Christ reconciling the world to Himself, not imputing their trespasses to them, and has committed to us the word	------------------------------ ------------------------------ ------------------------------ ------------------------------ ------------------------------

of reconciliation (2 Cor. 5:14–16, 19).

The Lord is not slack concerning His promise . . . but is longsuffering toward us, not willing that any should perish but that all should come to repentance (2 Peter 3:9).

> • *Have you ever been excluded from the service rendered by others? How did you feel?*

Principle #4: Commitment

Regardless of the degree of commitment to service that you may have made in the past—or lack of commitment—you can make a new start today. Ask God to forgive you for wasted opportunities to serve. Make a commitment to yourself to discover your talents and abilities that might be used in service. And then, make a commitment to get involved in the lives of others and to give, help, and provide as you are able. A real commitment is one that is acted upon, not merely one that is talked about.

Commitment is required if you are to endure in your service through tough times and persecution. Paul wrote to the Corinthians:

> If anyone builds on this foundation with gold, silver, precious stones, wood, hay, straw, each one's work will become clear; for the Day will declare it, because it will be revealed by fire; and the fire will test each one's work, of what sort it is. If anyone's work which he has built on it endures, he will receive a reward. (1 Cor. 3:12–14)

Make certain that what you do with your time, energies, and talents is for the gospel, and your work will be counted as gold, silver, and precious stones. It is what you do for your own self-serving interests and self-gratification that will be revealed as wood, hay, and straw.

What the Word Says	What the Word Says to Me
Commit your works to the LORD, And your thoughts will be established (Prov. 16:3).	_____ _____ _____
Commit your way to the LORD, Trust also in Him, And He shall bring it to pass (Ps. 37:5).	_____ _____ _____ _____
Only let your conduct be worthy of the gospel of Christ, so that whether I come and see you or am absent, I may hear of your affairs, that you stand fast in one spirit, with one mind striving together for the faith of the gospel (Phil. 1:27).	_____ _____ _____ _____ _____ _____ _____ _____

• *Can you cite times when you truly were committed to service, and times when you were not fully committed? What was the result?*

_____

_____

Principle #5: The Outcome Is God's

You are not responsible fully for the outcomes related to your service. Your responsibility is to serve God and others to the best of your ability, with the full force of your love, energy, and talents. What happens as the result of your service is God's responsibility.

The apostle Paul suffered greatly in giving service to the early church. His ministry was filled with conflict, struggles, and troubles. If you were to evaluate Paul's ministry on the basis of the number of times he was beaten, imprisoned, ridiculed and scorned, rejected, or assaulted, you would consider his ministry to be a total failure. The value of Paul's ministry, however, was not measured by what Paul went through, but by what God accomplished through Paul's consistent, persistent, and insistent preaching and teaching of the gospel of Jesus Christ.

It is God who saves souls; we merely do the witnessing. It is God who heals and restores; we merely do the "medicating," the praying, and the exhorting. It is God who delivers; we merely proclaim the power, the blood, and the promises made available to us through the name of Jesus. When we serve, God works. He uses everything that we do for His good purposes and eternal plan.

God calls us to be faithful. Our "success" is up to Him. Ministry is not something we do *for* God but, rather, something that God does through us. He is the One who calls us to service, enables us to serve, and produces His desired result from our service.

What the Word Says	What the Word Says to Me
[Jesus said] . . . "The Father who dwells in Me does the works" (John 14:10).	------------------------------ ------------------------------ ------------------------------
It is God who works in you both to will and to do for His good pleasure (Phil. 2:13).	------------------------------ ------------------------------ ------------------------------
He who calls you is faithful, who also will do it (1 Thess. 5:24).	------------------------------ ------------------------------

•*What new insights do you have into service and servanthood?*

_____

_____

• *In what ways are you feeling challenged in your spirit?*

_____

_____

LESSON 10

THE REWARDS OF SERVICE

God rewards service. Nothing that you will ever do in the name of Jesus for another person will go unrewarded by God.

As we stated in the introduction to this study, we must be very careful that we *not* count our salvation as one of God's rewards for service. Salvation of one's soul is *not* a reward for our goodness, our good deeds, or our service rendered. Salvation is a free gift from God, motivated solely by His love for us. It is a "grace gift" that we cannot earn and that is never linked to our personal merit (Eph. 2:8–9).

What *is* linked to our service are rewards that the Lord has for us, both in this life and in eternity.

Hebrews 6:10 tells us,

> For God is not unjust to forget your work and labor of love which you have shown toward His name, in that you have ministered to the saints, and do minister.

We should never be motivated in our service by the potential for a reward we may receive; our motivation should be thanksgiving and love for God and obedience to His command to love our fellow man. But as we serve, we can be assured that God always takes note of our service and He will reward it.

Our Reward Is from God

When we serve others, we truly are serving the Lord. No matter who the direct object may be of our service or how many individuals we may help, God says that the beneficiary of our service is Himself. Ephesians 6:6–8 reminds us that we are "bondservants of Christ, doing the will of God from the heart, with goodwill doing service, as to the Lord, and not to men, knowing that whatever good anyone does, he will receive the same from the Lord, whether he is a slave or free."

Because it is Christ we serve, it is from Christ that we can expect our reward for service. He is our Master, we are His bondservants. We should never look directly to the person we help for a reward or even for acknowledgment and recognition.

I learned this lesson early in my life as a young teenager delivering newspapers. Very few of the people to whom I delivered newspapers in the early morning, often before dawn, saw me. They simply counted on their newspapers being there when they awoke and desired to read them. It wasn't easy to get up early and do that job—I don't know a teenage boy who wouldn't rather sleep than bundle newspapers and then walk or bicycle a newspaper route. I did my job as unto the Lord, as if I were delivering *His* newspaper each morning. It was while I was selling newspapers on a street corner that a man came my way who was instrumental in my being able to go to college to begin my preparation to become a pastor. Was that an accident? I don't believe it was. I believe God was rewarding those many hours of faithful service delivering and selling. The man who provided the means for me to attend college was God's *instrument*. It was from God that I received my reward.

It is to our great advantage that our rewards come from God for two main reasons:

1. *God alone knows precisely what we need and when we need it.* He sees and anticipates our needs long in advance of our feeling or recognizing a need in our own lives, and He provides for us what is best for us.

2. God alone can give rewards that are eternal. What man can give to us is temporal. Material rewards rust, rot, and wither. Recognition and applause are fleeting. God, in contrast, gives us a deep inner and abiding fulfillment on this earth, as well as rewards that extend into eternity.

What the Word Says	What the Word Says to Me
Whatever you do, do it heartily, as to the Lord and not to men, knowing that from the Lord you will receive the reward of the inheritance; for you serve the Lord Christ (Col. 3:23–24).	-------------------------------
Do not lay up for yourselves treasures on earth, where moth and rust destroy and where thieves break in and steal; but lay up for yourselves treasures in heaven, where neither moth nor rust destroys and where thieves do not break in and steal (Matt. 6:19–20).	-------------------------------
If then you were raised with Christ, seek those things which are above, where Christ is, sitting at the right hand of God. Set your mind on things above, not on things on the earth (Col. 3:1–2).	-------------------------------

Rewards Come in Degrees

Not all rewards are alike. God rewards all service, but He does not give out equal rewards for all service.

We need to be very clear on this point: A job may be great or small from our perspective, but the act of service is what God sees and rewards. Service is service. God does not give differing rewards because one type of service is of greater or lesser importance than another. Rather, He gives differing rewards on the basis of *our heart motivation and our faithfulness in performing the service.*

In telling the parable of the talents, Jesus said that the Lord will say to the servants who used their talents to the fullest: "Well done, good and faithful servant; you were faithful over a few things, I will make you ruler over many things. Enter into the joy of your lord" (Matt. 25:21; also v. 23).

The servants in this parable were not rewarded on the basis of the number of talents they were given—in one case, five; in the other, two. They were not rewarded according to *how* they invested their talents; in fact, Jesus didn't even mention how they used their talents in order to double them. They were rewarded because they were "good and faithful" servants—they performed their service as well as they knew how to perform it, with a godly motive and intention of heart, and they were faithful in performing their service, diligent and persevering in it regardless of how they may have felt on any given day.

Jesus also differentiated in His teaching between rewards and *great* rewards (Matt. 5:11–12). Those who persevere in their service for the Lord in spite of persecution are subject to receiving a *great* reward. When Peter asked Jesus what reward he and the other disciples might expect from their faithfulness in serving the Lord, Jesus replied,

> Everyone who has left houses or brothers or sisters or father or mother or wife or children or lands, for My name's sake, shall receive a hundredfold, and inherit eternal life. (Matt. 19:29)

In Mark's account of this same incident, Jesus is recorded as saying that Peter and others who had left all for the gospel's sake and Jesus' sake would receive a hundredfold return *with persecutions* (Mark 10:29–30).

The more you are rewarded by God, of course, the more Satan will be upset about your rewards. The enemy of your soul has absolutely no interest in seeing you blessed or honored by God; he detests your prosperity in whatever form it comes—material, physical, emotional, intellectual, relational, financial, and especially spiritual. He will persecute you all the more as you receive greater and greater rewards from the Lord. The good news, however, is that the more you are persecuted for your witness about Jesus Christ, your reward grows just that much greater as you persevere in your faith and service! The devil's persecutions can never outdistance or overwhelm the outpouring of God's rewards on your life.

What we can be assured of when it comes to the size of our reward is that it will always be greater than what we give in the way of service. God multiplies our giving, no matter what form our giving takes.

Jesus gave a very famous parable about the multiplying effect of good seed that hits good soil. Often this passage is interpreted as relating to the preaching and teaching of God's Word, and certainly it does relate to that. The broader "word" of God, however, includes the unwritten word of our deeds. As Paul wrote, we are "living letters" about the gospel. What we do for others in the form of service is also a means of sowing God's "word" of love, mercy, and grace into the lives of others. As you read through this passage of Scripture, I encourage you to circle words and phrases that may stand out to you in a new way.

> Behold, a sower went out to sow. And it happened, as he sowed, that some seed fell by the wayside; and the birds of the air came and devoured it. Some fell on stony ground, where it did not have much earth; and immediately it sprang up because it had no depth of earth. But when the sun was up it was scorched, and because it had no root it withered away. And some seed fell among thorns; and the thorns grew up and choked it, and it yielded no crop. But other seed fell on good ground and yielded a crop that sprang up, increased and produced: some thirtyfold, some sixty, and some a hundred. (Mark 4:3–8)

When you give service to others, you are a sower of God's love and of the gospel of Jesus Christ. Regardless of how your service is received by others, and no matter how much Satan may oppose you in your service, at least *some* of your seed will fall on good ground. It will produce in varying degrees of reward: thirty-, sixty-, and a hundredfold. Who benefits from such a harvest? The sower.

Be encouraged in your service. At times you may see little or no progress in the lives of those you serve. You may feel as if all the good you are doing evaporates into thin air or is negated. God says that at least *some* of your effort will succeed mightily. God is the One who grows your harvest. Keep on sowing!

What the Word Says	What the Word Says to Me
Blessed are you when they revile and persecute you, and say all kinds of evil against you falsely for My sake. Rejoice and be exceedingly glad, for great is your reward in heaven (Matt. 5:11–12).	
With the same measure you use, it will be measured to you; and to you who hear, more will be given. For whoever has, to him more will be given; but whoever does not have, even what he has will be taken away from him. . . . To what shall we liken the kingdom of God? Or with what parable shall we picture it? It is like a mustard seed which, when it is sown on the ground, is smaller than all the seeds on earth; but when it is sown, it grows up and becomes greater than all herbs, and shoots out large branches, so that the birds of the air may nest under its shade (Mark 4:24–25, 30–32).	

Different Types of Rewards

Rewards come in different packages. Some are tangible and material. Luke 6:38 speaks of these types of rewards that God allows to be given to us during this life:

> Give, and it will be given to you: good measure, pressed
> down, shaken together, and running over will be put into
> your bosom. For with the same measure that you use, it will
> be measured back to you.

Not all rewards given from man are bad; many gifts that God desires to give to us are the gifts that other people will give to us. If someone attempts to reward you for service you have rendered, and the gift is moral, legal, and of benefit to you, the only remaining question to ask is: "How can I use this gift to benefit God's kingdom and bring glory to God?"

We each are responsible to God to give an accounting for our stewardship, which is how we use what we have been given by God and others. Paul wrote to the Romans: "So then each of us shall give account of himself to God. Therefore let us not judge one another anymore, but rather resolve this, not to put a stumbling block or a cause to fall in our brother's way" (Rom. 14:12–13). To the Corinthians, Paul wrote: "For we must all appear before the judgment seat of Christ, that each one may receive the things done in the body, according to what he has done, whether good or bad" (2 Cor. 5:10).

A person who gives you a good reward that is of benefit to you and to others in the body of Christ can be considered an agent of God's blessing. That person is God's *ways and means* of providing for you. Thank the person, but above all, thank God for the good reward that He has given to you.

Intangible Rewards

Men and women are also agents of intangible rewards: praise, admiration, recognition, acknowledgment, and appreciation. It is not wrong to receive a sincere thank-you, acknowledgment, or public form of appreciation from other people. What is wrong before God is when we serve God and others out of a desire to receive accolades from our fellow man. Jesus was very clear on this point, chiding the Pharisees for making a public display of their fasting, praying, and giving in order that they might appear to be righteous before men. Jesus said to them, "You have your reward." The Pharisees received the praise of others, but that was *all* they would receive. God was not in that reward.

There are times when God will bring to light what you do for others so that you might be an example and an encouragement to the body of Christ as a whole. In those cases, God knows that your motive for giving service was not to receive the praise of men, but He has determined that for His plan and purposes, He will make your good deed known. Jesus once healed a young man who was blind from birth, and when religious leaders asked Him what had caused the man's blindness, Jesus replied that the cause of the blindness was not the important thing but rather, "that the works of God should be revealed in him" (John 9:3). There are those who serve with a loving and thankful heart, with no thought for a reward, who are exalted to prominent recognition by God for this same reason—so that the works of God might be revealed through that person's life.

Each of us knows the personal satisfaction that comes from service when we see people helped. There is an inner joy that cannot be matched when a person accepts Christ and then makes a change in the way he or she lives and treats others. Any person who has ever served a drug addict or alcoholic who has turned away from drugs or alcohol, or who has ministered to an abuser who becomes a loving spouse and parent, or who has helped a young child in need to overcome a learning disability or physical injury, knows that God does give us intangible rewards directly and in great measure. We feel great joy and a satisfaction that cannot be quenched. Truly, "It is more blessed to give than to receive" (Acts 20:35).

Eternal Rewards

Still other rewards are eternal and will not be received until after we are in heaven. Jesus gave this teaching:

> When you give a dinner or a supper, do not ask your friends, your brothers, your relatives, nor rich neighbors, lest they also invite you back, and you be repaid. But when you give a feast, invite the poor, the maimed, the lame, the blind. And you will be blessed, because they cannot repay you; for you shall be repaid at the resurrection of the just. (Luke 14:12–14)

Some rewards will not be given to us until we are resurrected. We will be given eternal rewards according to

- the degree to which we have received the light of truth in our lives; we are not judged for what we do not know or cannot comprehend;
- our response to the opportunities for service that God gives us; and
- our motive and intent as we serve others—the state of our heart before God as we give and minister in His name.

The Bible refers to at least four types of crowns that will be given to us for our service:

1. An incorruptible or imperishable crown will be given to those whose hearts' desires have been rooted in obedience (1 Cor. 9:25).
2. A crown of life will be given to those who endure temptations, troubles, trials, and heartaches for Christ's sake (James 1:12).
3. A crown of righteousness is awarded to those who pour out their lives in service of the gospel (2 Tim. 4:8).
4. A crown of glory that does not fade away is given to those who "feed the flock" (1 Peter 5:4).

These crowns are not only ones that are given to us but also the ones that we in turn will rejoice to lay at the feet of Jesus in recognition that He has made possible anything we have accomplished for the kingdom of God (Rev. 4:10).

None of us can truly grasp the glories of heaven. Nor can we begin to imagine or understand all of the blessings that God may have for us in eternity. We have no capacity as finite beings to comprehend the infinite goodness of God. The rewards that the Lord has for us are immeasurable.

None of us can possibly know all of the people our lives have touched. Service to others has a "ripple" effect that goes beyond our ability to comprehend it. Each time I pick up an inspirational book written by a person who died several decades or even centuries ago, I am aware that this person has blessed my life and served me. God alone is capable of rewarding that person for the help he has rendered to me. God will judge and reward each of us for the *totality* of the service we have given, much of which may occur years or decades after we have died.

Conditional Rewards

Some of the rewards that we receive from God are conditional. They are directly related to our obedience. I encourage you to read Deuteronomy 28 to see what great rewards are made available to those who obey the voice of God and carefully observe all His commandments. A special reward is also given to those who are faithful in tithing (Mal. 3:10–11). Many of God's commandments are directly related to how we are to serve others; in the Old Testament, these commandments often relate to widows, orphans, and strangers. Other commandments are related to how we serve God through our giving, our sacrifices, and the things we do for our fellow believers. When we keep God's commandments to serve, we are rewarded. But when we disobey His statutes, we suffer loss.

What the Word Says	What the Word Says to Me
Whatever you ask the Father in My name, He will give you. . . . Ask, and you will receive, that your joy may be full (John 16:23–24).	-----------------------------------
I will . . . open for you the windows of heaven And pour out for you such blessing That there will not be room enough to receive it. And I will rebuke the devourer for your sakes (Mal. 3:10–11).	-----------------------------------
I command you today to love the	-----------------------------------

LORD your God, to walk in His
ways, and to keep His commandments, His statutes, and His
judgments, that you may live and
multiply; and the LORD your God
will bless you in the land which
you go to possess (Deut. 30:16).

Be faithful until death, and I will
give you the crown of life (Rev.
2:10).

Bless the Lord, O my soul,
And forget not all His benefits:
Who forgives all your iniquities,
Who heals all your diseases,
Who redeems your life from
destruction,
Who crowns you with lovingkind-
ness and tender mercies,
Who satisfies your mouth with
good things,
So that your youth is renewed like
the eagle's (Ps. 103:2–5).

All in God's Perfect Timing

God not only chooses the type and amount of reward we will
receive, but *when* we will receive certain rewards. As we just dis-
cussed, some rewards are immediate, some are in the future of our
earthly lives (such as the rewards of long life and grandchildren),
and still others are granted in eternity.

The concepts of "fullness of time" and "due season" are themes
that appear throughout the Bible. God has just the right time for
every reward to be granted so that it has maximum effectiveness
and benefit in a person's life, and also in the life of the larger body
of Christ.

Any person who knows anything about farming knows that crops have different growing seasons. After a vine cutting or fruit tree sapling is planted, it may not produce a full harvest for several years. Garden vegetables, by comparison, produce a harvest in a matter of weeks. Trees that are farmed for lumber may take decades to get to the harvest point. Grain crops take only months to produce a harvest.

Our role is not to *force* a reward or to insist that God give us a reward out of season. The younger son in the parable of the loving father demanded his inheritance out of season and ended up squandering it all (Luke 15:11–24). We are to trust God with patience (Ps. 37). A harvest *will* come, but it will be in God's perfect timing.

What the Word Says	What the Word Says to Me
Let us not grow weary while doing good, for in due season we shall reap if we do not lose heart. Therefore, as we have opportunity, let us do good to all, especially to those who are of the household of faith (Gal. 6:9–10).	
The kingdom of God is as if a man should scatter seed on the ground, and should sleep by night and rise by day, and the seed should sprout and grow, he himself does not know how. For the earth yields crops by itself: first the blade, then the head, after that the full grain in the head. But when the grain ripens, immediately he puts in the sickle, because the harvest has come (Mark 4:26–29).	
Commit your way to the LORD, Trust also in Him,	

And He shall bring it to pass.
He shall bring forth your righteousness as the light,
And your justice as the noonday.
Rest in the LORD, and wait
patiently for Him. . . .
The LORD knows the days of the
upright,
And their inheritance shall be
forever.
They shall not be ashamed in the
evil time,
And in the days of famine they
shall be satisfied (Ps. 37:5–7,
18–19).

•*What new insights do you have into service and servanthood?*

_____

_____

• *In what ways are you feeling challenged in your spirit today?*

_____

_____

EPILOGUE

A LEGACY OF SERVICE

What kind of legacy will you leave?

Each of us one day will have to give an account of our lives before God (Rom. 14:12). We will see our lives as an open book before the Lord, and we will be judged accordingly. What will count the most in that moment of eternity?

Each of us one day will die. Someone no doubt will offer a eulogy at our funerals. What will that person say?

The legacy that we leave behind us is largely up to our choosing. Very few great things are accomplished for God's kingdom by chance. We determine to a great extent the reputation that we have both while we are alive and after we have died.

Some people simply will leave a void in their passing. They were here, and now they aren't. They live, and they die. People who leave only a void are those who live for themselves. What they leave behind quickly evaporates.

Other people leave an *influence* in their passing. They make a difference in the overall direction and quality of the world in which they live. Their passing is mourned. Their remembrance is kept. These are the people who live for others—who choose to give of themselves generously. They are the ones who give the best they have, including their time, talents, and resources.

A life of service leaves a legacy of influence. The greater the service, the greater the legacy.

The way you serve others is the way you will be remembered on earth and the criterion upon which you will be rewarded in heaven.

Make your life count! Serve God with your whole heart, mind, and spirit today . . . and every day.

What does abandoning self concern and serving others look like?

Not advertising my freedoms or point of views. Speaking kindly encouraging and wisely. Not debating, not acting pious, not flaunting my blessings in the front of others. Being humble quiet and respectful. Pleasant joyful and a peace maker.

Mark 10:21